The Merrill Studies
in
Death of a Salesman

CHARLES E. MERRILL STUDIES

Under the General Editorship of
Matthew J. Bruccoli and Joseph Katz

The Merrill Studies
in
Death of a Salesman

Compiled by

Walter J. Meserve

Indiana University

Charles E. Merrill Publishing Company
A Bell & Howell Company
Columbus, Ohio

ISBN: 0-675-09259-0

Library of Congress Catalog Number: 79-171570

1 2 3 4 5 6 7 8 9 10–81 80 79 78 77 76 75 54 73 72

Printed in the United States of America

Preface

Who killed Willy Loman?

Who killed Willy Loman?
"Not I!" wept his wife, who hated strife;
  "Attention must be paid."

Who killed Willy Loman?
"Not I!" said one son; "When the deed was done,
  I was out with a girl I laid."

Who killed Willy Loman?
"Not I!" raged the other, and reviled his brother
  For the truth that they betrayed.

Who killed Willy Loman?
"Not I!" bragged Ben, "I believe in men
  And Willy was like an old maid."

Who killed Willy Loman?
"Not I!" snapped Howard. "Willy just soured.
  In business a spade is a spade."

Who killed Willy Loman?
"Not I," pleaded Charley; "His dream was partly;
  T'was a terrible role he played."

Who killed Willy Loman?
"Not I!" said Bernard; "Life is hard—
  If you can't walk away when afraid."

Who killed Willy Loman?
"Not I!" came the cry, from the crocodile's eye:
  Society's masquerade.

Who killed Willy Loman?
"Not I!" lisped his Culture, an insipid vulture,
    Stripping a corpse as it prayed.

Who killed Willy Loman?
"Not I!"   "No, not I!"   "Nor I!"   "No, not I!"
    Will attention ever be paid?

One problem with *Death of a Salesman* is that the viewer or reader has difficulty maintaining the social or moral distance that he seemingly requires for his personal comfort. Moved by the action of the play and disturbed by its ideas, he frequently has seen *Death of a Salesman* as a penetrating comment on modern man. From whatever part of the world he called home, he has felt the play's power, sensed its universality, even feared its personal grasp. The question—*Who* killed Willy Loman?—has always bothered him, although he has realized its limited value for serious and prolonged debate. Another question that haunted him is "*Why*?" This question also is not answered by Arthur Miller, although the playwright does stimulate one to ponder the idea a bit.

To ask the question "*Who* killed Willy Loman?" suggests that someone could be blamed for his death and that perhaps some kind of punitive or corrective action taken or an omniscient authority petitioned. The play then quite naturally becomes a case study for sociologists and psychologists whose interest in Miller's work has been bountifully demonstrated in essays and books. Their commentary, however, does not enlighten an audience concerning the play's value either as literature or theater. It is true, nevertheless, that Miller purposefully seduces the interests of both sociologists and psychologists—as a good dramatist should. Certainly one cannot escape Miller's concern for personal guilt and "blame" in *Death of a Salesman* or in most of his other plays. He is a writer vitally interested in modern society—particularly in the family and in the individual as units of that society.

To ask the question "*Why* did Willy Loman have to die?" immediately arouses the interest of the philosopher, while the question is also relevant for the literary and drama critic. Answers to this question suggest that the play deals with "being," the essence of man—*ecce homo*. They reveal not only the dramatist's ideas but, when related to the play's structure, also reflect its theatrical effectiveness. More than anything else Willy Loman wanted to be a man. Whether one sees his death as the death of a "salesman" or the death of a statesman makes no difference. For audiences, it has become the death of a man—dramatically expressed to make the rest of mankind wonder why.

To be interested in why death came or even to be interested in seeing it happen—as innumerable people have since the play was first produced more than twenty years ago—audiences must, consciously or unconsciously, find some personal significance in the play. Because, structurally, the play displays definite weaknesses, including a plot line held together by a belatedly raised question concerning "what happened in Boston" and confusion about dramatic discoveries, development of characters, and hero and villain relationships, one must assume that it is a character that attracts the audience's attention. Willy Loman! Just what kind of a fellow was he that he should demand the attention of theatergoers and thoughtful people for so many years?

When you start to assess a man and try to understand him, you ask what he believes and perhaps who or what he admires or dislikes. Almost immediately, one recognizes that, as a man, Willy Loman was neither distinctive nor impressive. He enjoyed working with his hands and was probably a fair carpenter, yet not sufficiently good or sure enough of himself to refrain from demeaning men who could not use their hands. He probably read little and was obviously not intellectually inclined as his attitude toward his sons' schooling demonstrates. If he had a dream or a "god," it might be described as "success": knowing what you want and going out and getting it. For him, this ideal involved showing initiative, being well-liked, making contacts and money. In parallel with his concern for success was his belief in his boys. It is a painful comment on man that Willy saw himself through them, particularly through Biff, and abandoned his own potential in his worship of their future. In contradiction to his own frequently expressed sense of individuality, he could not believe Charley's words that no man is worth more dead than alive. (Biff and Happy are, of course, different aspects of Willy which in Willy produced a personal torment that led to disaster.) For other reasons, other needs, Willy also admired his father and his older brother, Ben—neither man worthy of the admiration he gave, each one a different dream he had.

Knowing his beliefs, one can see the potential for misery in Willy Loman. Making him a sympathetic and meaningful hero is something else, however. Pry deeper into the man and one finds an unreasonable, unpredictable, confused, inconsistent, contradictory, often bitter, and disappointed man who could not accept his position in life. But there are reasons for all of this, and the fact remains that he was not always so. In his search for meaning and happiness in life, he never really knew himself, never saw the "sky" as Biff does because his grasp of social forces was as tenuous as his refusal to see the truth was recalcitrant in the extreme. Consequently, he was as much a man of superficially determined enthusiasms as of equally disturbing gloominess, with both qualities being revealed as he plunged psychopathically from one extreme to another, grasping with pathetic eagerness for a dream here and being cast down with overwhelming guilt there. He was really quite an impossible man for life in an adult society, and Charley voiced a general view: "Willy, when are you going to grow up?" As a man of respected years, Willy considered himself a man in mind and body; he thought or at least he thought that he thought. "I have such thoughts," he exclaimed early in the play; "I have such strange thoughts." But all of these were simply dreams of the past, feelings of guilt, dread of the future, visions of self-pity. Study Willy Loman carefully and one finds a person whom hypocritical society does not willingly accept as representative man but one with many of the characteristics that man sees around him in his society, if not in himself. It is this discovery which provides the basic fascination of the play.

Arthur Miller once wrote that he considered calling his play "the inside of his head." But if one considers the "inside of his head" as suggestive of a view into Willy's mind, it really isn't worth much of an effort. Although Charley once asked Willy, "What the hell is goin' on in your head?" it was something of a pointless question. Quite truthfully, Willy's head didn't function too well. His mind flitted here and there with a constant inconsistency that can bewilder a careful reader. On reflection, it is not Willy's head that interests men but his heart, that latchstring of his being which transfixes the viewer's attention. It is true that Willy lost rational control, but as "a little boat looking for a harbor," which is how Linda described him, he was worthy of pity, sympathy, attention. He meant well; he tried hard; he loved and he erred; and he talked too much, joked too much, was fat and lonely.

Like most men, Willy was his own worst enemy, guided by emotion rather than intellect, dreams rather than reality. "If you can dream and not make dreams your master," the poet wrote. But the poet didn't describe what would happen if you failed—only what happened with success. Man, however, has learned the bitter consequences of failure and subconsciously fears for himself what he sees in others. In this respect, Willy's speech and action reflected some of these fears as they suggest a condition of modern man.

The play's appeal, Willy's appeal, seems deeply rooted in one of Willy's statements about his own life: "I still feel—kind of temporary about myself." This is a statement that most honest men can make, or might have made about themselves at one time. Dramatically, of course, it is the opposite of his dream of knowing what one wants and going out and getting it and of, essentially, knowing himself and being able to fulfill his needs and desires. The dream, obviously, is not new, nor is it meaningless: Know thyself! With his plea, however, so pathetically and realistically related to his dream, Willy Loman becomes much more typical of the lost, alienated, guilt-ridden, dream-oriented individual endlessly spawned by modern society. And as such, he becomes an object of both pity and fear. The fact that he believed in all the wrong things, admired the wrong people for confused reasons, taught his boys the wrong ideals, built his life upon corrupt dreams—all of this is all the more fearful in a world where such beliefs are advertised, such ideals are openly extolled, and such dreams are constantly glamorized. There is a bitter truth in the view that both jails and the New York Stock Exchange are filled with "fearless characters." Guided by such momentous and respected forces of conventional success, cultural dreams, and ambitions unrelated to ability or reality, Willy was doomed. Hoping for his sons' success, Willy was also doomed by what he had passed on to them. But was he to blame for dreaming, for wanting "something" in the ground, for refusing to be "a dime a dozen," for avoiding unpleasant truths? And where do such desires put the rest of man?

The scene that Miller employs for his first act reinforces the theme of identity that he wants to impress upon his viewers. There is everywhere the "air of the dream," "a dream rising out of reality." A melody is played which suggests "grass, trees and the horizon." There is the past and the present to be enacted, with all showing the superficial grip that men have upon reality. The "angular shapes" that surround the Salesman's house, however, suggest the nightmare quality both for those who refuse to recognize reality and those who look around themselves carefully. Imposed upon this background, Miller has created a character who wanted to face life truthfully, wanted to be a successful man. But he had the weakness of many men, and he failed. Why? Should attention be paid? Does anybody "dast blame this man"?

Obviously some people do, and they are those who find Willy Loman as much a fraud as Biff claims he was. Others do not. The purpose of this collection of essays is to provide some of the various approaches to Arthur Miller's *Death of a Salesman*. Some critics have considered the play a modern tragedy; others have seen only its social significance. There have been interesting analyses of the various characters in the play as well as studies of the structure of the play and its language. Most of the collected essays show distinctive critical attitudes, and if they are not all equally impressive, this fact simply may dramatize the thoughtful concern of the reader. One certainly should not be intellectually seduced by every view of this play. One should, however, note the popular and academic acceptance of *Death of a Salesman* as recognition of the play as a world-wide, understandable view of modern man. Theodore Dreiser's novel *An American Tragedy* was no more American than Swedish. Miller's hero can also claim numerous citizenships.

Contents

1. The Reception

2. As Social Problem

3. As Tragedy

4. Characters

5. Style

1. Reception

John Gassner

The Theatre Arts

Two of the biggest guns on Broadway sounded off in February. Arthur Miller, the talented young author of the novel *Focus* and the Drama Critics Circle prize play *All My Sons,* reappeared on the stage with his best effort to date, *Death of a Salesman.* Clifford Odets, the white hope of the theatre of the 1930's, returned after many years of incarceration in Hollywood in a decidedly slashing mood with *The Big Knife.*

The ecstatic reception accorded *Death of a Salesman* has been reverberating for some time wherever there is an ear for theatre, and it is undoubtedly the best American play since *A Streetcar Named Desire.* Now it is two new playwrights of more than provincial significance, Arthur Miller and Tennessee Williams, that America can boast of as part of its postwar contribution to the theatre. Many of us would find it difficult to determine which of them is superior. A decision is hardly urgent at this time, and it is too soon perhaps to arrive at one while they are both still at the starting points of their respective careers. At present, it would appear that Tennessee Williams is the more creative artist but is in some danger of exhausting his particular theme of frustration. Miller is endowed with greater objectivity and comprehension of contemporary life but is limited in verbal talent and drawn toward the commonplace by a moralistic tendency. Williams is the truer poet; Miller, the better sociologist.

In *Death of a Salesman,* however, Miller has managed to rise above the ordinary flatlands of moralization and thesis drama. His play is a consummation of virtually everything attempted by that part of the theatre which has specialized in awareness and criticism of social realities. It is a culmination of all efforts since the 1930's to observe the American scene and trace, as well as evaluate, its effects on character and personal life. Clifford Odets succeeded in this enterprise more than creditably in *Golden Boy* and movingly, if somewhat dimly, in *Awake and Sing* and *Rocket to the Moon.* Generally our "social" playwrights' efforts, however, stressed the scene rather than the character even when they transcended special pleading or political agitation. Miller's achievement lies in successfully bridging the gulf between a social situation and human drama. The two elements in *Death of a Salesman* are, indeed, so well fused that the one is the other.

Death of a Salesman succeeds, in truth, as its author himself appears to have realized, as a character drama and an exceptionally good example of so-called "middle-class tragedy." It follows the fate and final reckoning of a

Reprinted from *Forum* (April, 1949), 219-22, by permission of *Current History,* Inc.

commonplace man in a commonplace environment. It is the kind of play that usually falls decidedly short of tragedy and settles on the lower level of pathos, a drama ordinarily conducive to tear-shedding or sympathetic clucking rather than to exaltation of mind and spirit through impressive suffering. That this is not conspicuously the case in *Death of a Salesman* is perhaps the ultimate proof of its author's dramatic powers.

Other playwrights of his generation could have matched the verity with which he renders a traveling salesman and his family. They, too, could have depreciated the success-worshipping commercial traveler's "smile and a shoe-shine" philosophy. Miller alone has made the object of his analysis a breathing man and given him some stature. His hero, Willy Loman, may commit errors and may flounder in illusions like the rest of his clan, worshipping material success and thinking that it is bound to be won by sales talk and Rotarian chumminess. Willy may believe that you are worth nothing that you cannot sell and may instill the same notions into his sons. Willy may have the usual fling at extramarital diversions that seem to be the custom of commercial travelers on the loose. But Willy is not quite commonplace in his commonplaceness. He maintains his faith, inane though it be, with a tenacity that is little short of heroic and when it crumbles, the man crumbles with it. The ordinary mirage that he follows is made extraordinary by the fervor of the man who is in pursuit of it; there is an element of the sublime in his näiveté! When he falls, we note the toppling of a giant; at the same time, we reflect that he was no brighter than other giants who figure in fairy tales hardly more fantastic than those Willy created for himself and mistook for the American Dream. There may be nothing remarkable in his disappointment in his sons, for whose vices and shortcomings he is at least partially responsible. Yet, disappointment has a tragic dimension in his case because he feels it greatly. His love for them had been too intense, his hopes for them too high. In his relations with them, he is almost a King Lear in mufti. He is closer to Shakespeare's or at any rate to Turgenev's "King Lear of the Steppes" than he is to Balzac's masochistic vermicelli-manufacturer, Goriot. The truth is that Willy Loman is cast in the heroic mould because he can feel greatly, even if his thinking could be bounded in a nutshell. And for this reason, he not only fills the dramatic scene substantially himself but adds substantiality to his well-drawn wife and sons. They gain substance from the magnitude of his relation to them, the magnitude being in himself.

Miller's technical virtuosity also stands him in good stead. He has a flair for tight construction, in itself only a second degree virtue, which becomes a virtue in the first degree because it gives him both the assurance and the skill to break the conventional mould of realism. The play shuttles numerous vignettes back and forth in time, but it gives an impression of inevitable cohesion—the cohesive demonstration of a man's mistakes. It is the summation of a man's life that would normally be presented as a chronicle, a horizontal kind of drama, but it becomes instead a spiralling affair. It starts with Willy Loman returning home instead of going away on another business trip, because he can no longer trust himself to drive a car. His story ends with his committing suicide in order to leave his family his insurance and to repair his personal failure. His past weaves through other episodes that carry the drama forward from the initial to the final point. Past and present move forward together, illuminating one another, and mounting in intensity. Reminiscences of Willy's errors as father, husband, and human being counterpoint his immediate difficulties with his sons and his employer.

In a production brilliantly staged by the genius among American directors, Elia Kazan, the play acquires the texture of music and the dynamics of a dramatic elegy. Misbegotten dreams that turn into nightmares hurl themselves at the bar of fate in wave after wave on Jo Mielziner's skeletal and many-leveled setting. The production defines areas for acting imaginatively rather than literally. At different times, portions of the space in front of the eviscerated Loman home become a suburban backyard, a Manhattan restaurant, a hotel room in Boston, and a cemetery, with the family and a friend standing by the freshly dug grave of Willy. The lighting and the incidental music by Alex North add fluidity and expressiveness to the proceedings. The actors are so maneuvered that their reality as people remains inviolable without contradicting or hampering the free-wheeling quality of the dramatic action in time and space. This constitutes modern staging in the highest degree, without pretentious estheticism and with complete persuasiveness.

The actors are exceptionally well chosen. If Lee Cobb's Willy Loman is too heavyfooted and portentous, if he resembles a monolith at times, he nevertheless possesses stature as well as statuesqueness. He is both the "Willie the Weeper" of popular song, staggering in the opium fumes of success-dreaming, and a giant threshing about in a snare of his own making. Set against him is the solid bourgeoise Charley, the kind but blustering neighbor. He is Willy's Horatio, and Miller is to be commended indeed for not making Willy stand for the whole of our middle-class life. Howard Smith plays Charley with recognizable humanity and with spirit, and also gives an external portrait that recalls the sensible burghers of Flemish and Dutch painting from whom he and his tribe can trace their descent. "Happy," played by Cameron Mitchell, is the son who incorporates Willy's *insouciance.* He is one of the many recognizable young men who will be found clerking, philandering, and swaggering, who do no particular harm but also no particular good. Biff, the other son, spoiled by Willy's indulgence, which encouraged him to steal and to expect much from the world because he played football at school, is the dislocated youth. He tries to free himself from delusion, his own and his father's. Having idealized his breezy father, he is shattered in spirit when he finds him entertaining a strange woman in a hotel room. His story is almost as moving as the father's, and Arthur Kennedy's Biff is even better realized than Lee Cobb's Willy. Set against both sons is the physically unimpressive Bernard, Charley's bright lawyer son, whom the Lomans set down as a negligible boy because he was studious and scrupulous. In Don Keefer's portrayal of the lad will be found the recognizable features of many young men who do not conform to the ideal of strenuous youthfulness that so often turns out the hollowest of men. The saloons are full of Loman boys while the professions are full of Bernards. Perhaps the best job of acting, however, is Mildred Dunnock's Linda, the Loman wife and mother who understands all and suffers all, the *mater dolorossa* of Brooklyn and of a substantial portion of the rest of the country.

Undoubtedly *Death of a Salesman* is one of the triumphs of the mundane American stage. It moves its audience tremendously, it comes close to their experience or observation, it awakens their consciousness, and it may even rouse them to self-criticism. As a text it is, in many respects, the latest version of *Babbitt*. The subscribers of the Book-of-the-Month-Club, which has selected a play for the first time in its history, may put the book on their shelves as an authentic piece of American fiction along with the novels of Sinclair Lewis, Theodore Dreiser, and James Farrell. Whether it is actually the great play that many people believe it to be is another matter. I can only register a general doubt here. For all my enthusiasm, I would not place the play in the same class with, let us say, *A Streetcar Named Desire, The Glass Menagerie, Desire Under the Elms,* or even *The Iceman Cometh.* It is deficient in the poetry, the nuances, the wonder, and the unexpected insight of truly distinguished dramatic literature. Mr. Miller's insights are all expected ones; they are observations rather than discoveries.

In the last analysis, *Death of a Salesman* is still *drame bourgeoise* rather than high tragedy. Mr. Miller's story still possesses more qualities of demonstration by a sociologist than of transfiguration by a poet. The contrast of characters is rather schematic, and the moral obtrudes upon life instead of emerging with shimmering suggestiveness from the contradictions of human nature. Mr. Miller's depths are actually shallows, even if he navigates them superbly. Anyone who is familiar with *Death of a Salesman* and wants to arrive at a perspective, should not miss the March 5 issue of *The Nation* in which Mr. Joseph Wood Krutch, the most penetrating dramatic critic in America, sets down some provocative reservations. Qualifications are, however, less important from the immediate point of view than the fact that the American stage has *Death of a Salesman* to show for a year's effort and that Mr. Miller himself has surpassed his *All My Sons* in breadth and humanity.

If *Death of a Salesman* is a triumph of talent, Odets' *The Big Knife* is a failure of genius. Mr. Odets' case must be reserved, however, for the next issue for reasons of space, along with questions concerning other plays including John Golden's revival of Sidney Howard's *They Knew What They Wanted.*

Harold Clurman

Theatre: Attention!

"Attention must be paid to such a man. Attention!" The man his wife refers to is Willy Loman, the central figure of Arthur Miller's "Death of a Salesman." Perhaps the chief virtue of the play is the attention that Miller makes us pay to the man and his problem, for the man represents the lower-middle-class, the $50-a-week-plus-commission citizen, whose dream is to live to a ripe old age doing a great volume of business over the telephone. It was not unusual to hear of this person in the thirties, but in the theatre of the forties he has once more become the forgotten man.

The play has tremendous impact because it makes its audience recognize itself. Willy Loman is everybody's father, brother, uncle or friend; his family are our cousins; "Death of a Salesman" is a documented history of our lives. It is not a realistic portrait; it is a demonstration both of the facts and of their import. "We had the wrong dream," says Biff, Willy Loman's son, and what Miller is saying in terms few can miss is that this wrong dream is one the greater part of America still cherishes.

"The only thing you got in this world is what you can sell," the prosperous man next door tells Willy. This is the harsh fact, but Willy, the poor dear fellow, is not satisfied with it. He wants to be *well-liked.* It is natural and healthy to harbor this desire, but the philosophy of Willy's economic situation denatures this desire to the hope of being well-liked or "known" as a way to security, success, salvation. To be a "personality" is to cultivate those traits which make one sufficiently "well-liked" to do a greater volume of business so that one may achieve a brighter place in the sun.

The competition Willy encounters is too tough for his modest talents; the

---

Reprinted from *Lies Like Truth* (New York: The Macmillan Co., 1949), by permission of the publisher. Copyright © 1949, 1958 by Harold Clurman. Also published in *The New Republic,* CXX (February 28, 1949), 26-28.

path he has chosen denies his true being at every step. He idolizes the dream beyond the truth of himself, and he thus becomes a "romantic," shadowy nonentity, a liar, a creature whose only happiness lies in looking forward to miracles, since reality mocks his pretensions. His real ability for manual work seems trivial and mean to him. "Even your grandfather was more than a carpenter," he tells Biff. From this perpetual self-denial he loses the sense of his own thought; he is a stranger to his own soul; he no longer knows what he thinks either of his sons or his automobile (he boosts and denounces them both in almost the same breath); he cannot tell who are his true friends; he is forever in a state of enthusiastic or depressed bewilderment. "That man never knew who he was," Biff says of him. He never owns anything outright till his death by suicide (committed to give Biff a foundation of $20,000); he has never been free.

His sons suffer the guilt of the father: Biff, the older, with increasing consciousness; Hap, the younger, stupidly. Hap seeks satisfaction as a coarse ladies' man. Biff cannot find any satisfaction because, being more trusting and sensitive than his brother, he tries to live according to his father's dream with which he has nothing in common—the boy yearns to live on the land. Only toward the end does Biff discover the spiritual hoax of his father's life, the corruption of heart and mind to which his father's "ideals" are leading him. With his father's death, Biff has possibly achieved sufficient self-awareness to change his course; Hap—like most of us—persists in following the way of his father. He will go on striving "to come out No. 1 man." . . . The point of all this is not that our economic system does not work, but that its ideology distorts man's true nature. Willy's well-adjusted neighbor "never took an interest in anything" and has no aspiration beyond the immediately practicable.

Arthur Miller is a moralist. His talent is for a kind of humanistic jurisprudence: he sticks to the facts of the case. For this reason his play is clearer than those of other American playwrights with similar insight whose lyric gifts tend to reject the more elusive and imponderable aspects of the same situation. There is poetry in "Death of a Salesman"—not the poetry of the senses or of the soul, but of ethical conscience. It might have been graven on stone—like tablets of law. "Death of a Salesman" stirs us by its truth, the ineluctability of its evidence and judgment which permits no soft evasion. Though the play's environment is one we associate with a grubby realism, its style is like a clean accounting on the books of an understanding but severe sage. We cry before it like children being chastised by an occasionally humorous, not unkindly but unswervingly just father. "Death of a Salesman" is rational, dignified and profoundly upright.

Elia Kazan's production conveys these qualities with a swift and masterful thrust—like a perfect blow. He has cast the play admirably, and the entire occasion might be cited as an example of real theatre: meaning and means unified by fine purpose. Lee J. Cobb, who plays Willy Loman, is surely one of the most powerful and juicy actors on our stage today. He displays a tendency in this part to sacrifice characterization to a certain grandiosity. Willy Loman's wife speaks of his exhaustion, and Willy himself refers to his having grown fat and foolish-looking. None of these textual indications is taken into sufficient account, and what is gained in general impressiveness is lost in a want of genuine pathos.

Indeed the tone of histrionic bravura tends to make the others in the cast—for instance, Arthur Kennedy, the beautifully sensitive actor who plays Biff—push a little too hard. The production therefore pays for its virtues by a lack of intimacy, which is the dimension needed to make the event complete. Mildred Dunnock, in her simplicity and delicacy of feeling, is like the symbolic beacon of everything sound in the production. Tom Pedi, as a waiter, is as real and tasty as a garlic salad; Hope Cameron, in the smallest role in the play, suggests a remarkably touching naïveté. Both have a specific reality that I should have liked to see carried through all the longer parts. But virtually everyone in "Death of a Salesman" is better than good; and the whole marks a high point of significant expression in the American theatre of our time.

Dennis Welland

Death of a Salesman in England

Death of a Salesman is currently prescribed in England as a text for the Advanced Level examination (roughly the equivalent of high school graduation, and the basis of university selection). The introduction of twentieth century texts into this syllabus is relatively recent, of American texts even more so, and usually not more than one American title is in the syllabus for

---

This essay was written expressly for this volume by Professor Dennis Welland, University of Manchester, England.

any one year. Miller's play has thus some claim in this country to the status of a modern classic. Such a cachet of respectability might seem the kiss of death to a play that one still thinks of as innovatory and remarkable. Discussing it recently with audiences of seventeen- and eighteen-year-olds, I realized with something of a shock that none of them was even born when the play was first staged. Given their generation's exaggerated criterion of 'relevance,' what would a play more than twenty years old have to say to them? Would it have acquired already the patina of a period piece, or would it have merely a fictitious topicality as an indictment of materialism, and American capitalist materialism at that? In fact, they seemed to take its Americanness quite effortlessly in their stride, to have very little inclination to see it as propaganda, and to prefer instead to discuss it as a story of human suffering which had clearly affected them, and as a fascinating piece of stagecraft. They were uncertain whether it fell within the strict definition of tragedy, but reluctant to allow an academic definition to falsify their own emotional response to the play. Their attitude seemed a healthy one and probably a fairly reliable index to the present-day British view of a play which has gradually come to be respected and liked—even, in its own phrase, to be well-liked.

Death of a Salesman reached London a little over five months after its New York first night. It opened at the Phoenix Theatre on Thursday 28 July 1949, to mixed but generally favorable notices.[1] One reviewer found it anomalous

---

[1]An exhaustive summary of these notices, journal by journal, would be tedious, confusing, and repetitious. I shall instead try to give a general impression, particularizing as necessary. In assembling the material for this essay I have been greatly helped by Miss Elizabeth Leach of the Manchester Central Reference Library, to whom I am most grateful. The following, in chronological order of publication, are the notices consulted: the letter preceding each will hereafter be used in the text to identify the source of each quotation in order to minimise annotation and avoid repetition.

(*a*) *The Times,* 29 July 1949, p. 9.

(*b*) *The Manchester Guardian,* 30 July 1949, p. 5; initialled "P. H-W." [Philip Hope-Wallace; see also (*g*) below.]

(*c*) Ivor Brown, *The Observer,* 31 July 1949, p. 6.

(*d*) Harold Hobson, *The Sunday Times,* 31 July 1949, p. 2.

(*e*) Peter Fleming, *The Spectator,* 5 August 1949, p. 173.

(*f*) T. C. Worsley, *The New Statesman and Nation,* 6 August 1949, pp. 146-47.

(*g*) Philip Hope-Wallace, *Time and Tide,* 6 August 1949, p. 792.

(*h*) Eric Keown, *Punch,* 10 August 1949, p. 163.

(*i*) *Sphere,* 13 August 1949, p. 247.

(*j*) J. C. Trewin, *Illustrated London News,* 27 August 1949, p. 320; see also (*m*) below.

(*k*) *Theatre World* (September, 1949), pp. 9 and 29.

(*l*) *Theatre World* (October, 1949), pp. 11-18 inclusive; provides a summary of the play's action, with photograph illustrations.

(*m*) J. C. Trewin, *Drama* (Winter, 1949), p. 8.

(*n*) F. Sladen-Smith, *Drama* (Winter, 1949), p. 30; review of Cresset Press text of the play.

that "the strongest play of the New York theatrical season should be transferred to London in the deadest week of the year"; it was, he thought, "a revelation of the extent to which anything American is assured of success" (*b*). (He probably had in mind the fact that *The Heiress* was doing well at the Haymarket and *Oklahoma!* was in its third year at Drury Lane.) The play, he reported, had been "very well received" though he himself was a little disappointed with it. Evidently its reputation had preceded it: press notices used such phrases as "eagerly awaited" (*h*) and "much-heralded" (*k*), while one sourly observed that "the raptures of New York and the build-up over here inevitably introduced [it] almost as if it were a piece of holy writ" (*c*). A grudging note in some of the reviews certainly supports the suspicion of chauvinistic hostility to an import, but on the whole they were not markedly unfair and the mixed feelings engendered by the play were responsibly discussed by most of them. Even if lukewarm about the play, most responded warmly to the production.

There was unanimous, and often enthusiastic, praise for Jo Mielziner's "skeleton set and selective lighting" as Eric Keown described it (*h*); he added, "Usually I dislike seeing the whole of a house laid bare on the stage, but here imagination and good theatre-sense have triumphed." It was Keown, too, who struck another keynote in remarking that "Mr. Elia Kazan makes a highly complicated production seem extraordinarily natural:" one or two found it in some respects portentous, but there was general agreement that, in the establishing of the play's mood, Miller had been as well served by his producer as by his designer. There was also general satisfaction with the individual performances: *The Times* thought it "beautifully produced . . . and meticulously well acted," and some critics seemed to imply that the high standard of acting was almost better than the play merited. The word to which all of them sooner or later had recourse is "moving." Even those who disliked the play were prepared to recognize the strength of its assault on the feelings of the audience, though one of them recorded with satisfaction, "I did not have to reach for my handkerchief once" (*f*).

The ideological aspect, however, has engaged far less attention here than in the United States where Eric Bentley saw the play as a potential tragedy deflected from its true course by Marxist sympathies, and Eleanor Clarke claimed it as a Marxist play vitiated by "an air of universality" and "intellectual muddle": "What used to be a roar has become a whine."[2] To several English reviewers it was something of a morality play with Willy as "'Everyman' once again, in our day and generation, more blind than ever to the real spiritual values of life" (*k*), but it did not strike them as a Marxist or

---

[2] For a fuller discussion of this see Dennis Welland, *Arthur Miller* (Edinburgh & London: Oliver and Boyd, 1961), pp. 51ff.

even a left-wing morality. There are several possible explanations of this. Differing national attitudes towards communism at that time might be adduced. The name of Elia Kazan was less well-known here than it has since become, and less well-known than in America: both he and Lee J. Cobb, who created the role of Willy Loman, had been in the original cast of the 1935 Group Theatre production of Clifford Odets's *Waiting for Lefty,* a circumstance which, coupled with Miller's connection with the Federal Theater Project, may have predisposed some Americans to expect a play more redolent of the thirties than an English audience would expect. Two years later Audrey Williamson was to recall that Kazan and Cobb had both been in the 1938 London production of Odets's *Golden Boy*: she had evidently been much impressed with that play and with the work of the Group Theater, which she discusses briefly, but no London reviewers in 1949 made this connection.[3]

Cobb, of course, was not in the London production. Willy was played by Paul Muni, an actor already popular here and one with whom there were no associations of this nature. *The Times* captioned its photograph of the play "Mr. Muni's Return" and several reviews approached it primarily as a vehicle for him. It has been observed of this period that in England

the actor was a dominant figure in the theatrical polygon of forces and the playwright was much less influential than he had been in the 1930's. This shift in the balance of forces occurred not only because commercial managements found star performers more and more necessary, but also because no commanding dramatist emerged in the 1940's, and revivals rather than new plays were the order of the day during the war and ten years after it.[4]

The preoccupation with the star is illustrated by one of the few really disparaging notices the play received (one by J. C. Trewin and reproduced in its entirety):

Death of a Salesman, Arthur Miller's American play at the Phoenix, was almost the death of a critic. Happily, Paul Muni is in the cast to play the little salesman with a pathetic belief in his worthless son, and his vigor and humanity help to relieve an evening that is otherwise tangled, pretentious, and dull, It is, however, a commercial success (*m*).

Muni's performance may have had a very far-reaching effect on the whole concept of *Death of a Salesman* in this country, for several critics who had

---

[3] Audrey Williamson, *Theatre of Two Decades* (London: Rockliff, 1951), pp. 165, 181-82.
[4] William A. Armstrong, ed., *Experimental Drama* (London: G. Bell, 1963), p. 23.

seen the New York production emphasized radical differences between his interpretation and Lee J. Cobb's. The point was most fully developed by Harold Hobson both in his initial review and in 1953 in a retrospective, book-length study of the theatre from 1949 to 1952:

> Mr. Cobb's Loman was a man rejoicing in his enormous vitality, and quite unaware of his essential uselessness, the realization of which came upon him at the end as a shattering and incomprehensible paradox. Mr. Muni's performance, on the other hand, was that of a sad little chap beaten from the start, pushed around by life and his fellows, pathetically incompetent, touching and exasperating by turns. Mr. Cobb took the play along with splendid drive, but hardly ever unsealed the springs of pity. Mr. Muni was frequently moving, but occasionally became a bore.[5]

In 1949 Hobson had been a little more sympathetic, observing that "on at least five occasions Mr. Muni brings the entire audience close to tears" and "in the supreme moments of his performance Mr. Muni could not be surpassed" (*d*). Other critics had detected some restlessness in the audience, and one thought the play could with advantage have been "cut by twenty minutes and taken considerably faster" (*c*). To Philip Hope-Wallace in New York it had seemed "something comparable to an American *King Lear*" (*b*) but this comparison with the London production made him "regretfully withdraw" (*g*). This was partly because, unlike Cobb, Muni did not seem to feel that it was Willy's "illusion (even as Lear's illusion of kingship) which made him big by his own lights and makes his fall tragic" (*g*). Yet, as Audrey Williamson was to point out, "Willy's 'success' is a mirage that deceives no one but himself, and Muni's crushed nervousness had a poignant reality."[6]

In fact, this was the aspect of the character most calculated to attract a British audience, characteristically disposed to sympathy with the "little man." Eric Keown's description of it as "a deeply understanding study of a once happy family torn to pieces by forces outside its comprehension" (*h*) puts the priorities as most of the commentaries tend to. *The Times* felt that "this massive and relentless play" falls into two halves, of which the first shows "the straits in which an unnatural civilization places natural man," and "the second, and much better, half of the play" concentrates on the father/son relationship with a sense of the tragic which "amply makes up for the overwhelming accumulation of detail with which the dramatist prepares for it." Remembering the London production of *All My Sons* a year earlier, several reviewers discussed *Death of a Salesman* as a reexamination of a parallel theme against "a much larger background, the tragic pressures of a

---

[5] Harold Hobson, *The Theatre Now* (London: Longmans Green, 1953), p. 125.
[6] Williamson, *op. cit.*, p. 182.

breakneck civilization on the soul and mental stability of the ordinary small citizen" (*h*). They could identify with this ordinary small citizen and their tears were for him; with the "breakneck civilization" they could identify much less easily. It was for them a "background" just as *The Times* referred to the play's "sinister background of American materialism." This emerged with unattractive smugness in one hostile notice: "I could not help wishing that Mr. Miller had used satire and not sentiment in his approach to a way of life whose standards and atmosphere are really—to those at any rate who are not yet in danger of having to live that way—a matter for laughter rather than for tears" (*e*). Cobb's Loman might well have encouraged anyone with these prejudices into a total distortion of the play's values.

I had, I confess, expected to find much more of this anti-Americanism in these notices. Ivor Brown thought the applause of "hard-boiled Manhattan audiences" was "an easy form of penitence for what a Wee Willy Loman would find coming to him if he called round for a job next day" (*c*). Both Brown and Philip Hope-Wallace thought British audiences would have responded to the theme better had J. B. Priestley dramatized it, but Hope-Wallace "in no priggish mood," suggested that if "the moral is for Americans" and "our withers are unwrung" this was because of "our very weakness" that we do not share Willy's success-ethic and his "longing always to be liked" (*g*). As recently as April, 1970, a reviewer of a revival of the play at Bolton could still describe it as a difficult play to produce in England "because the sense of brute push and tensions is never quite so strong in England as in the U.S., the 'law of success' and concomitant death or failure is not quite so fatally ingrained."[7] Illusions die hard, but this contrast between the two civilizations might seem much less marked in 1970 than it did in 1949, and my teen-age audiences did not seem to need to make any allowances for the play's Americanness. They seemed to find, as did one 1949 reviewer, "a disturbingly personal flavour; there is so much of this tragic salesman in all of us" (*n*). The father/son tension, which British audiences have always seen as the play's focus, has of course nowadays become even more relevant as "the generation gap" and a "problem of communication."

The play's idiom is also more accessible today than it was in 1949, and for several interesting reasons. To have opened in 'the deadest week of the year' might have proved less of a handicap to *Death of a Salesman* than to have opened in London in that particular year. Although in retrospect 'no commanding dramatist' is seen to have emerged in that decade, at the time two dramatists were claiming a lot of limelight and verse drama appeared to be enjoying a renaissance. Less than a month after the opening of Miller's play, *The Cocktail Party* had its premiere at the Edinburgh Festival.

---

[7] *The Guardian*, 1 April 1970.

Christopher Fry was in the ascendant, too. When *Death of a Salesman* opened, John Gielgud was starring only a few hundred yards away in *The Lady's Not for Burning.* Six months later came the premiere of *Venus Observed* with Laurence Olivier. When the London stage was luxuriating in this riot of imagery and echoing Fry's Mendip—"What a wonderful thing is metaphor!"—it is perhaps surprising that Miller's more quotidian language even gained a hearing. The "Dramatic Notes" in *English,* for example, in 1949 and 1950, extolled Eliot and Fry as the hopes of the future and made no mention at all of Miller.

One review of *Death of a Salesman* was entitled "Poetry without Words"; it saw the play as "an attempt to make a poetic approach to everyday life without using poetry—or even heightened speech. The characters are to remain as inarticulate as they are in real life . . . the production, in short, is expected to do most of the work of evoking the heightened mood" (*f*). Though conceding that "this play, episodic and rambling as it is, has a certain power, . . . creates a world and takes us in it," and though paying generous tribute to Kazan's brilliance of production, it concluded that nothing is "an adequate substitute for the words which just aren't there." I recall myself and a colleague sharing this sort of disappointment with the play's language at a good provincial repertory production in December 1950. Miller himself was subsequently to counter this criticism of the play's language by saying of Willy "that he had not the intellectual fluency to verbalize his situation is not the same thing as saying that he lacked awareness."[8] At the time, however, we were more susceptible to the opposite argument as formulated by the poet-dramatist Ronald Duncan: "it is the function of the theatre to express, not merely what a character would say in a given situation, but what he might say if he were given a poet's power of expression. For the danger, if we are not able to express our inmost feelings, is that we may very probably in time cease to feel them."

Tone-deafened by verse-drama and familiar with strictures on the inadequacies of the American language in the theatre of Eugene O'Neill, we did not immediately recognize the range and subtleties of Miller's effects, but we were not alone in that. Even in American criticism the sensitive use of colloquial idiom and speech rhythm for literary effect had not yet been dignified with the title of "the vernacular tradition." Indeed, in 1953 Harold Hobson recalled that "the glittering Mr. [George Jean] Nathan" had faulted the play "on the ground of its ordinary speech, in which he saw no tragic grandeur."[9] Hobson's 1949 review thought it a play "of enormous distinction" but made no special point of the language. By 1953, however, he was

---

[8] Arthur Miller, "Introduction to *The Collected Plays* (London, 1958), p. 35.
[9] Hobson, *op cit.,* p. 122.

speaking of it as "beautifully and movingly written, eloquent, yet perfectly within the common American idiom." He praised particularly the tenderness of the "Requiem" and its rhythm, and remarked that "not many dramatists have written speeches that drive harder at the heart, or are more memorable" than Linda's "attention must be paid" speech.[10]

By 1954 Kenneth Tynan was calling the play "Miller's triumph in the plain style; it rings with phrases which have entered in to the contemporary subconscious." The English poetic revival, he suggested, seemed hollow and retrogressive in comparison with the "craggy candour" of Miller's dramatic prose.[11] That revival has now receded so far that a British reviewer in 1968 could complain of *The Price* that its dialogue "doesn't seem to be as eloquently contemporary as *Salesman's* was in its time, nor as sharply economical."[12] Those qualities were there, but were certainly not fully recognized in 1949.

The play's structure was also imperfectly understood initially. T. C. Worsley thought "the episodic time-switching and place-switching" was a concession to audiences who really preferred the cinema; it resulted merely in "dispersing the tension, which then needs to be laboriously built up again time after time." (*f*) *The Times* spoke noncommittally of "an ingenious arrangement of scenes"; for J. C. Trewin, "Miller has handled cunningly his play's odd construction with its curious here-and-there, now-and-then interweaving of scenes" (*j*). Ivor Brown was again contemptuous: "This sort of episodic, hither-and-thither design (or lack of design) makes for easy playwriting: problems of construction vanish" (*c*). Eric Keown thought that, though "such juggling with time can be tiresome," in this case the "frequent dips into the past are so smoothly managed that the main flow of the story towards its tremendous climax is never checked" (*h*). Similarly, in 1951, Audrey Williamson observed that "This playing about with chronology can be curiously effective in the theatre,"[13] but nobody explored fully the nature of that effect.

Death of a Salesman, then, had to contend in England with some anti-American feeling, though less than might have been expected; with some reluctance to entertain the possibility of the first "commanding dramatist" of the undistinguished 1940's coming from America; and with an uneasiness about its idiom and its form that was also felt in the United States. Partly because of Paul Muni's rendering, partly because of the audience's reaction, it may be suggested, in Philip Hope-Wallace's phrase, "that the play itself is

---

[10] *Ibid,* pp. 121-23.

[11] Kenneth Tynan, "American Blues," in *The Modern American Theater,* ed. Alvin B. Kernan (Englewood Cliffs, N.J.: Prentice-Hall, 1967), pp. 37, 36.

[12] W. J. Weatherby in *The Guardian,* February 1968.

[13] Williamson, *op. cit.,* p. 181.

transformed" (*b*) and our version is subtly different from the American. Yet, for all the differences of opinion, Miller has become a respected and honored dramatist in England, largely because of the impact of this play; the revival of it recently in Bolton played to more than 80% audiences (by no means all "A Level" students).

Since the 1950's, critical discussion of Miller in this country has increased steadily; indeed, I may be allowed to mention that the first full-length study of his work was English—my own, first published in 1961 and reprinted several times; one chapter is devoted to *Death of a Salesman*. British criticism of the play has in general followed two main lines of inquiry: *Death of a Salesman* as tragedy, and social realism in *Death of a Salesman*. In 1962 Norm Fruchter traced, along lines different from mine, Willy's claims to the stature of tragic hero; and Bamber Gascoigne summed up the play as "an admirable blend of pathos and satire" but denied it tragic dimensions because Willy's "driving illusion is one we do not respect. . . . He evokes pity. But he cannot evoke terror."[14] In 1967 Eric Mottram examined the play more searchingly: for him Willy is the victim of "a 'phoney dream' and it is the American dream;" Miller's plays are "not tragedies but plays of partial awakening to fate before a conclusion in suicidal waste."[15] Mottram, in short, directs the discussion back to "the drama of social questions" as Raymond Williams had done in 1959. Williams's essay is important for its discussion of the play as "a development of expressionism, of an interesting kind."[16] In this, Albert Hunt followed him, but found it "a powerful but uneven play, which reveals a certain amount of unresolved conflict between concept and form."[17] More recently C. W. E. Bigsby has also drawn attention to the play's limitations while praising it for "delivering American drama from the mindless passion of previous decades" and establishing a drama that finds "its animus in metaphysical enquiry."[18] Less iconoclastically John Prudhoe, while praising the play's successful experimentation with form, has argued that this could not be transferred to other plays because "the play is essentially Willy Loman himself, and though Willy is universally representative in many ways, in one

---

[14]Norm Fruchter, "On the Frontier: the Development of Arthur Miller," *Encore* (January-February, 1962), pp. 17-27; Bamber Gascoigne, *Twentieth Century Drama,* (London: Hutchinson & Co. Ltd., 1967), p. 177.

[15]Eric Mottram, "Arthur Miller: the Development of a Political Dramatist in America," *Stratford-Upon-Avon Studies, 10: American Theatre* (London, 1967), pp. 127-61, especially pp. 133-38. The essay is reprinted in Robert W. Corrigan, ed., *Arthur Miller* (Englewood Cliffs, N.J.: Prentice-Hall, 1969).

[16]Raymond Williams, "The Realism of Arthur Miller", *Critical Quarterly,* vol. I, no. 2 (1959), pp. 140-49, especially pp. 144-46.

[17]Albert Hunt, "Realism and Intelligence: Some Notes on Arthur Miller", *Encore* (May-June, 1960), pp. 12-17.

[18]C. W. E. Bigsby, *Confrontation and Commitment* (Columbia: University of Missouri Press, 1967), pp. 32-36.

important aspect he is a highly specialised figure . . . Willy's mental processes are so disturbed that for him past and present have the same kind of reality."[19]

Thus to insist on the play as "essentially Willy Loman himself" and on Willy's mentally disturbed condition is to emphasise the Muni interpretation rather than the Cobb and to reinforce my suggestion that there are perhaps two plays, the British *Death of a Salesman* and the American. Both are the "massive and relentless play" that *The Times* first thought it, but the one is a moving story of human failure, the self-destruction of a little man, the other an examination of a national success-ethic and its implications for an ordinary, though not necessarily little, salesman.

[19] John Prudhoe, "Arthur Miller and the Tradition of Tragedy," *English Studies,* vol. XLIII, no. 5 (October, 1962).

Robert Abirached

Allez à Aubervilliers

After *Andorra,* a merciless autopsy of the anti-Semitic phenomenon, the theatre of Aubervilliers now presents *Death of a Salesman,* a tragedy of the human being in the universe of free enterprise. Gabriel Garran certainly does not make up his repertoire at random. Without confessing to any school, he made it his business to talk to his spectators about themselves and the civilization that rises up around them. Both plays are new to the French public and are quite similar in that they make use of symbols understandable to everyone, and they solicit thinking about exemplary situations. It is impossible to remain indifferent to what happens on the stage, when each detail is an allusion to your own life and the problems you face in actual society.

Indeed, the public of Aubervilliers and elsewhere cannot but recognize itself in Willy Loman, this perfectly trite salesman, promoted to the dignity of a tragic hero. His personal description resembles millions of others: sixty-three years old, inhabitant of a big city, good father and husband (not to be too particular), completely occupied by his profession, a regular life even in the

Reprinted from *Le Nouvel Observateur,* no. 27 (May 20, 1965), 32-33, by permission of Georges Borchardt, Inc., Literary Agency. Translated for this work by Josee Duytschaever. In February, 1952, Parisians had an opportunity to see the play as performed by the Belgian National Theatre of Brussels on tour in Paris.

little frolics that enliven it. Lots of dreams, yet decent ones. To his two grown-up sons, especially the eldest, Loman has transferred all his sustained ambitions; he already sees them rich and respected, thanks to the docility they will have displayed in listening to his good counsels.

As to the rest, he cannot get enough occasions to glean some dollars left and right: the washing-machine has still to be paid for, as do the refrigerator, the house, the Chevrolet. For him there will never be an end to recapitulating his debts. A prisoner of all these objects that will fall to pieces before ever fully belonging to him; a slave of publicity at the moment it reinforces its base flattery to court him; his "rentability" and self-confidence decrease with each day he grows older.

This is where the drama bursts forth: Loman is dismissed. The façade of respectability which he had erected so laboriously collapses at the same blow, and the failures that had long been dissembled brusquely appear in broad daylight: his two sons have not been successful at all and never will be. Why not? Loman does not ask: he has confidence in society and the iron law that rules it. Success is always there, and it is too late to convert to new ideas. One solution is left to give some lustre to this miserable life and to allege the only justification for it that Loman admits: to commit suicide, disguise his death as an accident, and thus enable his wife and his sons to collect the twenty thousand dollars insurance that will permit them to begin again.

All this is portrayed by Miller at the moment when the storm breaks loose in Loman's mind: hence a coming and going of dreams, memories, and actual events, all being Willy Loman's conscience that had to be translated to the stage simultaneously. André Acquart's setting was pretty helpful, although it did not succeed well enough in passing on from one register to another. In the same way Gabriel Garran's *mise en scène* is more solid than inventive, though with due precision it throws light on the true sense of the debate, I mean the responsibility of the social order in the destruction of this man who is crushed by the machine he defied. To be just, it must be added that Miller's play is somewhat too talkative in its first part and that here the major defect of *After the Fall* is already apparent—the anxiety to say and to do too much about the matter—whereas an allusive technique would often have been more effective.

The breakdown

Apart from this shortcoming, however, the work is not inferior to the ambition that conceived it; it is a modern tragedy, in the strict sense of the term, in that it shows the unbearable tension that is created between a human being and the society that molds him, until the moment when the break-down occurs, bringing to light a terrible truth indeed. Willy Loman deserves a place amongst the heroes of our time, victims of their mortal ingenuity, and one will be no less likely to forget him since he will be associated with the lunar face of Claude Dauphin, with his detached silhouette, his candid and dazzling voice. Around this great actor Hélène Bossis, Gérard Blain and Pierre Santini interpret their parts with success. Rome is not situated in Rome any longer; that becomes clear enough. Go and make sure for yourself tomorrow in the théâtre de la Commune of Aubervilliers.

Friedrich Luft

Arthur Miller's *Death of a Salesman* Hebbel - Theater [Berlin]

Play, problem, production, interpretation—during the season which is now coming to a close we have had five times the good fortune of the unusual, justifications for the fact that first-rate theatre can be brought here. This night can be reckoned amongst the most important and successful. As the curtain dropped before the intermission there was a breath-taking stillness in the Hebbel-Theater, until the applause broke loose, already taking the proportion of an ovation after the first act. At the end it was impossible to get the audience to leave the theatre. Calls for Kortner, for Johanna Hofer, for Käutner and the entire extraordinary ensemble in this extraordinary play. Another proof that it can be most fortunate to be in the theatrical city of Berlin and to be allowed to visit the theatre. A great evening.

It was an important event as far as the play is concerned. Here a young American, Arthur Miller, has heard threatening signal knocks in the social machinery. In a very lucid critical approach to society he investigated the matter by means of a dramatic narrative. He has taken to heart the fate of the simple salesman, Willy Loman. Something is wrong, so he ascertains, when such a man has to die as he does, driven by anxieties of advancing old age, and on account of his gray hair expelled from the ranks of those who are permitted to live well. Here is imminent danger. It is already present. Look at

Reprinted from *Stimme der Kritik—Berliner Theater seit 1945* (Velber bei Hannover: Friedrich Verlag, 1965), pp. 82-85, by permission of the publisher. Translated for this work by Josee Duytschaever.

this Loman—good-natured, confident, optimistic in our perhaps exaggerated way. But he has two boys, loves them, wrongs one of them while loving excessively and monkey-like. A salesman, a small representative, he has been on the street for forty years, selling, beaming as it suits his profession, offering hosiery up and down the big country. Now he is getting old, able only with exertion and convulsion to sustain his "Keep Smiling" approach. He falls back. His sales quota sinks. His existence is threatened. He is dismissed. He is destroyed. He commits suicide, failing to hold his petty social position. The installment of the refrigerator. The repair of the Ford. The payment of the life insurance. He cannot make it any longer. Such a life cannot be right. It was only partly Loman's guilt. It is the fault of us all. Signal knocks in the social machine. Arthur Miller makes his meaning clear enough with one example.

How should this Loman have acted, however? Should he rather have done like his ruthless and pushing brother Ben? As a seventeen year old this one made his way through the jungle of the most rabid business life, free from the impediments of conscience and dreams of an upright life. At the age of twenty-one he emerged again. Rich and successful. There is no doubt as to the color his hands have been since. But he managed to do what the more honest Loman never ventured, encumbered as he was by his basically decent heart and the scruples of his respectability. Brother Ben wears precious stones, watches the clock, and is bound to go on with his bloody hands. He is one who deals out the blows. Loman belongs to the others. He is cut down. This play is an elegy on the "unsuccessful." It is a signal knock. A sign on the wall. A warning directed to us from the stage. A play of the present time. Poetry of the actuality, critical, full of social sensitivity, accusal and unmasking, and already helpful as well as utterly indispensable because it is so unmistakably revealing. A beautiful play with the particular melody of contemporary poetry capturing this elegy on the obliteration of a species of today's little American man. In Broadway at the world premiere of the same play I saw hard-boiled New York businessmen weep their eyes out. I do not mean to take weeping in the stalls as a proof of a play's quality. Rather on the contrary. However, I found it comforting when one of those crying next to me said to his wife: "Damn it, that's exactly right! Think about Dad! Something ought to be done. There's something we must change. We must do something!"

Not the crying—that was what Miller wanted.

The Berlin production is almost better even than the one in New York, where it has been creating a Broadway sensation for eighteen months now. For one thing the Berlin creation is more important because here it takes greater pains to get acquainted with what is familiar over there. Whereas Miller had only to tap the American spectator lightly on the shoulder for him to participate creatively, the audience here has first got to cope with the difficulty of establishing such an association. This could not halt the dramatic flow, however. The unity of place within the numerous unexpected time changes—which are obtained through flash-backs, dream visions, and a cleverly constructed setting—is maintained with less effort in the Berlin production by the legitimate use of the revolving stage, absent in New York. The drama has its due course. In a dreamlike fashion again and again, it stretches back to the danger-centers of the past in the existence of the little Loman. Intelligently and smoothly it blends its spheres. And yet it keeps sticking firmly to the character and fate, the exemplary and scandalous disintegration of the good-natured man Loman. Fritz Kortner interprets the part. There had been a justifiable fear that his massive personality would tend at once to crush and to accentuate unduly this character of a nonentity as is basically to be represented here. That did not happen. Kortner remained quite little so to speak and hence demonstrated an admirable greatness of acting talent. The straightened, helpless man, given wings by a fatal imagination of "success," clinging to his suddenly rising dreams to work his way up into emptiness, more brutally flinging down on his face as the real failures increase in number and proportion, until his truly tragic fate is accomplished. Kortner enacts the part wonderfully, showing the exemplary pathological case with seeming easiness and great force.

Wonderful by his side: Johanna Hofer. How truthful and direct her motherly tones! How she interprets the fate of this man Loman in an even more serious and tragic manner, being as it were the knowing mirror, fully aware and seeing through the situation. How she delivers the final epilogue at the grave! How in one of the most terrible scenes she tears the veil of foolish doting upon the sons to pieces to prove to them their cruelty with strong and direct speech. Scene after scene. In each one of her stage appearances— wonderful. A very great actress.

Who would ever have thought that such capacities lay hidden in Fritz Tillmann, as they came to the surface here in the part of the beloved son? Flexible, lovable, touchy, dangerous, seized with a vacillating love-hate towards his father since he had found him in the arms of a stranger in a small Boston business-hotel. And apart from this, through the risky flash-backs into full youth, Tillmann also hits the indifferent swinging attitude which is so typically American. Of the same quality is Kurt Buecheler, the uncomplicated, far colder brother. A good-for-nothing amongst the New York girls of easy morals, likelier born for a wicked victory in such questionable unfeeling business-life. Another corrupt creature of his false environment. Buecheler acts casually, without disclosing how great an effort it was to complete the mosaic.

Ernst Schroder appears in an episode which he fills with almost cruel humoristic strokes. Next time he should be given a broader opportunity to try his talents. What he has already put forth here was precisely in his thoughtless dangerousness quite obtrusive and colorful in an intelligently subtle way.

Eduard Wandrey plays the friend of the salesman Loman, settled, free from the latter's overbearing longings and dreams. Again he presents an accurate color-spot on this remarkably American scene. Herbert Hübner is brother Ben in the inserted dream sequences, the man who went into the business-jungle and came back rich and blood-stained. He, too, hit the mark with his idle, purely mercantile bustle. Berta Drews is the compact short sin in the Boston business-hotel. She magnificently characterizes the ladylike vulgarity of such existences without any exaggeration or harshness.

The director Helmut Käutner has conveyed this elegy of a little man with intelligent poetry. On the restless turntable he made an admirable use of Friedrich Prätorius's efficiently designed setting. The arrangement was seemingly effortless, and yet it was the result of a steady labor on a project that was well worth the effort. It is a good thing that Käutner was able to prove his talent here with a great drama. Kurt Heuser's stage-music was congenial, supplying a lyrical or menacing background for the dream sequences. The uncommonly thunderous applause was aimed at the whole of the production. But in particular at Kortner, Hofer, Tillmann, and Käutner.

Theatre—and this, in fact, was the most encouraging, the most comforting thing about this remarkable performance—theatre not as a means of propaganda, not as an extended arm of a preconceived thesis, but theatre as argument, as a most provoking forum of public questioning, as a sign on the wall, as protest and most vivid argument, an eye-opener and a warning, an elucidation of the present time. That which at last invigorates our museum institution of a self-satisfied theatre of education, that which makes it rebellious and indeed reestablishes its true function. Not a nimble and shallow actuality theatre. But poetry of this day. Go and see.

Rajinder Paul

Death of a Salesman in India

First of all, let me confess to a handicap. It is practically impossible for any one person in India to know of, let alone keep abreast with, what is happening or has happened in the various regional dramas. India has fourteen major languages and all manner of theatrical performances are being staged in all of them. Scores of adaptations and translations are done every season—some put on stage, some just got ready at an enterprising publisher's behest and bound everlastingly between covers for a school or college syllabus. Regional secrets remain ensconced in regional breasts. And it is not uncommon for a regional translation to be retranslated into the language of the original and offered as a genuine masterpiece for national delectation. The jokes often recoil—as only recently the Press had to remind the author of a played-up Marathi play, imported with all fanfare to Delhi, that the Delhi critics had, unfortunately, seen its original in the film *Fanny*.

There is, thus, great clashing of regional egos. An article on the almost unborn Oriya that *Enact* (a drama monthly that I edit) received from a well-known literary figure writing in that language made it sound as though the rest of India was comparatively in the dramatical backwoods and that Oriya drama could even teach the rest of the world a thing or two. One has learned, however, to take such regional flutters with a pinch of salt. After all, Indian drama is not in a very happy state, and if some mute, inglorious Miller there may rest, it should not be too difficult to seek him out.

To my knowledge, Arthur Miller, or more particularly his *Death of a Salesman,* has had only an indirect influence on Indian theatre practitioners. It does seem a little odd though, since Tennessee Williams, Beckett, and even Albee seem to have influenced Indian playwrights. The realistic playwright's model seems to be Ibsen; but it is Williams for the revolutionary ones, Albee for the sadistic uncovering of the inbred quarrels of seemingly undivorceable middle-class couples, and Beckett for the chosen few ever ready to jump intervening atmospheres and establish intellectual rapport with the aid of a kind of literary Telstar.

Theatre in India is without a base, that is to say, without a rich tradition to fall back on. Or, if there is one, as some might insist, what with the great Sanskrit drama listed in *Companions to World Theatre,* it is, for most practitioners of theatre in India today, far too heavy a load! If one may be allowed to jump from these thoughts, one fails to see why the Indian equivalent of a playwright like Miller cannot be found. As I see it, Miller's

This essay was written expressly for this volume by Mr. Rajinder Paul, playwright and editor of *Enact,* Delhi, India.

grand themes—the themes of guilt, responsibility, family fealty, and man-hood—are themes so close to the actually male-dominated society in India that they should find a ready echo. Though India has its Khajurahos and Konaraks that its expatriated sons returning to their 'areas of darkness' would find more salacious than *Oh! Calcutta!* in New York, sex or its frank discussion, whether it is perverse or just plain, has still a ring of super-ficiality; and intimate, personal problems (post- or pre-Freud) have never been the core of expressed Indian thought. The all-too-common middle-class virago would rather be seen in her classical costume and coiffure in the auditorium and foyer than be discussed on stage. This is perhaps a problem for the psychiatrist which, of course, very few playwrights are willing to be, afraid of being dubbed terylene precipitates on a "glorious heritage."

There is a dominant streak of Puritanism in the Indian mind, a streak which, I fear, is also dominant in Miller. Maybe it has something to do with his Jewish background with the inveterate mother-figure at its centre. There is thus great identification available to the Indian milieu in Miller's plays—at least in his early plays like *Death of a Salesman,* and *All My Sons*—before he discovered the other dominant female figure, the wife and mistress, in plays like *After the Fall,* though he still sticks to his oeuvre—guilt, responsibility, and morality.

Ostensibly, as everyone knows, *Death of a Salesman* is an indictment of American society, its values of materialism, consumerism, the desire to fill your life with washing machines, cars, and kitchen ranges and catch up, instantly, with the Joneses, bartering that life, in the process, to the buy-now-pay-later hidden persuaders. It is not buying life but death in installments. And yet, criticism of society is too easy a pastime. The tragedy is that seeing where all this leads to and given the world one lives in, one is incapable of making a less unscrupulous choice. If like an Indian ascetic one goes to live upon a mountain, he is still "dropping out." Hardly a fingerpost for the rat race of little men that most of us are involved in. The achievement of Miller is that he is the first truly tragic writer not to use the classic model of tragedy: his Willy Loman is a nondescript, unattractive little man who is nevertheless a great tragic figure. Of the four or five great American dramatists—O'Neill, Williams, Wilder, and possibly Albee—Miller is far and away the greatest in this respect.

Of all Miller's plays that have been performed in India—*All My Sons, After the Fall, Incident at Vichy, View from a Bridge*—*Death of a Salesman* has been the most popular both as Theatre and in book form. Almost everyone who has been connected with theatre after the partition of India and Pakistan (an arbitrary but undeniable watershed for modern Indian drama) has seen or read this play. Hardly anyone I know is in disagreement about its claim to being a modern classic of world drama. Its first production I have come across was the critically well-acclaimed one by the Theatre Group in Bombay, under the direction of Pearl Padamsee in February, 1967. Leslie de Noronha, writing in *The Examiner,* a Catholic weekly from Bombay, was so moved by it that he had to add an italicised personal note. In the six years that he had been reviewing national and international theatre, he had cried only three times, once when seeing Peggy Ashcroft in *Hedda Gabler,* the second time seeing Laurence Olivier in *The Entertainer,* and then when he saw Myrna Moos as Linda in *Death of a Salesman.* "Artistic triumph, tour-de-force, whatever other critics call it, this review is written with the word 'superb' as my base-line adjective; anything less will make me a peasant in my self-estimation." The play, I think, ran for about fifteen nights. The trouble with an amateur group such as this one is that all its members, being highly placed in social life, half desire their plays to fold after a couple of nights to make their evenings free. But it is a fact that the Theatre Group's productions are very polished, neat and well-acted. Their earlier production of *The Crucible* was a similar triumph.

Besides Myrna Moos's Linda and Alyque Padamsee's Willie, the highlight of the play was the expressionistic set designed by R. S. Pillai. It consisted of vertical steel girders, symbolizing Willie's skyrocketing dreams, that locked the family in a cage. The unevenly spaced horizontal ropes were meant to underline the fallibility of the rope-ladder to the top. It might or might not be out of place to mention that most of the Theatre Group's members are in the highly competitive world of selling—they are either clients or PR men or accounts executives. I suppose there was a lot more than mere identification with the central theme of the play.

Harpal Tiwana, a graduate of the National School of Drama in Delhi, also did a two-nights production of *Salesman* in Hindi, which was universally described as an amateurish one. A Bengali production by a group called Chaturmukh, which was brought to Delhi recently, was also not well-received critically. It was an adaptation and not a translation. The author, Mr. Asim Chakravarty, produced it in 1964, and it has since had over 150 performances, which might indicate its popularity in Bengal. Mr. Chakravarty says: "*Death of a Salesman* is unique in one respect, that everyone, somehow, somewhere, finds himself identified; and therein lies the success of the play." There is no doubt of that. Willie, Happy, Biff, and Linda will definitely find echoes in many hearts and families. In fact, I once thought and still do that the best way to do *Death of a Salesman* is to adapt it in any of the regional languages of India; or, if it is to be done in English, it ought to, for maximum impact, have Indian names, preferably Parsi. Change Willie to Peerbhoy and Boston to Bombay and the play will have a scarifying effect.

Mr. Anil Kumar Mukherji, a Bengali playwright, producer, and actor, did,

Death of a Salesman in English, Hindi *(Ek Salesman ki Maut)*, and Bengali
(Akjan Salesmaner Mritu) in April, 1968. In the course of three years or so,
the three productions have had thirty-five performances—three in English,
fifteen in Bengali, and seventeen in Hindi. He says he had heard of the play
when it was running in London and New York in 1951 and got hold of its
book in 1953. After establishing the Bihar Art Theatre in 1961 (the Tagore
Centenary Year), he ventured to do this play and give a taste of serious
modern drama to his uninitiated audience, mostly fed on folk theatre.
According to him it was a success as far as that could be in a practically
audienceless city. "The play indeed had a profound influence on me as a
playwright. . . . I consider myself as belonging to the school of thought to
which Miller belongs, and this is the reason why Mr. Miller unhesitatingly
accepted honorary membership of the Bihar Art Theatre. As a playwright I
confess that my play *Assam Mail* (in Hindi and Bengali) owes a lot to his
Salesman, although its theme is quite different."

There must be other such playwrights that I don't know of. But one thing is
certain: of all American dramatists, modern or not, Miller is the best known
in India, and his *Death of a Salesman* the most popular play.

Miller's achievement is that he is still socially committed when commitment
carries a pejorative ring. His nexus remains the family, the micro-unit of
society. Surrounded by the hostile in society, he thinks that if loyalties
remain in the family, one can, as an organism, face the world with courage,
love, adventure, and humaneness. That is why all his plays deal with family
problems. And that is why Willie is so worried about his love for Biff, and
why he dies happily when he discovers Biff still loves him. It is another matter
that he dies in the vain optimism that, like an elephant, he would be more
useful to the family when dead. It is also another matter that the father's
desire to perpetuate his name and leave an impression that will survive him
has a streak of masochism and egotism about it. But, then, don't these selfish
motives form an integral and bittersweet part of human nature? Willie and
Ben return in the form of Victor and Walter in *The Price,* or, to continue the
posterity, as Biff and Happy.

Though Miller is socially committed to good, sensible living, he is a very
sophisticated writer. Most of his idealism seems cancelled out, whether it is in
Salesman or *The Price*: there are no easy routes to success, liberal-minded-
ness, or honor. The temptation to do otherwise, as an experienced writer
would know, is big. And life, as Miller knows, is not without its compromises.
Thus, mercifully, Miller doesn't exonerate any of his protagonists, whether it
is Willie or Quentin or Victor. Nor does he simplistically accuse his
antagonists. Anybody can sermonise, few write drama. And very few so well
as Miller. And, I suppose, when the West returns to its traditional values of
honor, morality, and loyalty, after sucking dry the already running-out

fashions of selfishness and meaningless sex, it will rediscover Miller. India, I suppose, would do better, although it may seem ironic, to form a base for its growing theatre around the social realism of Miller's plays. The progress of this theatre will depend to a large extent on the emergence of our own Millers.

2. As Social Problem

Barry Edward Gross

Peddler and Pioneer in *Death of a Salesman*

Although much has been written about *Death of a Salesman,* the use to which Arthur Miller has put the American frontier tradition—especially the motifs of peddler and pioneer—has not been sufficiently discussed.

First of all, Willy Loman thinks of himself as, in his own right, a pioneer:

WILLY. When I went north the first time, the Wagner Company didn't know where New England was.[1]

This characterization of Willy as pioneer is not sarcastic or ironic. It is consistent with the small scale of Willy's life that his frontier is not, say, the Northwest Territory but—quite literally, in the salesman's jargon—the New England Territory. However, such a frontier is not enough for Willy. He must try to create a literal one:

WILLY. It's Brooklyn, I know, but we hunt too.
BEN. Really, now.
WILLY. Oh sure, there's snakes and rabbits and—that's why I moved out here. Why, Biff can fell any one of these trees in no time! (Act I, p. 158)

But why should it be necessary for Willy Loman, an easterner, in the nineteen-forties, to create a frontier in the backyards of Brooklyn? Why should he feel the need to be a pioneer? If the answer were only that Willy is an American and that the frontier is a significant force in the American consciousness, then the play would not be nearly so effective and Willy would not be nearly so moving. True, Willy Loman *is* a contemporary Everyman—or, at least, Everyamerican—but he must also be, at the same time, a particular human being, if *Death of a Salesman* is to be anything more than a dissection of a national disease. No, Willy Loman must need a frontier for particular, as well as universal, reasons.

The father-son relationship is one of the major motifs in *Death of a Salesman.* In addition to the most important relationship between Willy and his sons, there is neighbor Charley and his son Bernard, and Willy's dead boss Wagner and his son Howard. But it is too frequently forgotten that Willy, too, has a father. And it is his father, the exemplar of the Yankee peddler, who

Reprinted from *Modern Drama,* VII (February, 1965), 405-10, by permission of the journal and of A. C. Edwards.
[1] *Arthur Miller's Collected Plays* (New York, 1957), p. 133. Subsequent page references are to this edition.

helps to explain, in large part, Willy's need for a frontier and to suggest some of the reasons for Willy's failure:

BEN. Father was a very great and wild-hearted man. We would start in Boston, and he'd toss the whole family into the wagon, and then he'd drive the team right across the country; through Ohio, and Indiana, Michigan, Illinois, and all the Western states. And we'd stop in the towns and sell the flutes that he'd made on the way. Great inventor, Father. With one gadget he made more in a week than a man like you could make in a lifetime (Act I, p. 157).

And it is certainly true that some of this spirit survives in Willy. He, too, wanders a territory peddling wares. But they are not his own wares made with his own hands. Nor can he choose his own territory: Willy has started and ended in Boston. The fault is not Willy's: given the tradition in which he was raised, Willy Loman is simply in the wrong place at the wrong time. A man can no longer wander the country selling what he makes with his own hands. If a man is to be peddler, he cannot, as his father was, be pioneer as well.

Willy can boast of his heritage and his pioneer tradition—

WILLY. My father lived many years in Alaska. He was an adventurous man. We've got quite a little streak of self-reliance in our family (Act II, p. 180).

—but the self-reliance of the Yankee peddler is useless to the modern peddler. Willy's world places value on getting along with others, not on getting along on one's own. One source of Willy's failure is his inability to apply the values of his father's world to his own, the impossibility of being both peddler and pioneer, and of realizing the eternal creativity that "pioneer" suggests to Willy.

Willy might have been different if his father's values had not been passed down to him so indirectly. It is quite easy for Ben to simply walk off into the wilderness in search of his father. Ben, a teen-ager at the time of his father's desertion, knew his father well. He was tutored in the frontier tradition, and he had a living example to follow. But Willy was not yet four when Ben walked "away down some open road" to find his father in Alaska. It is impossible to speculate on what sort of influence Willy's mother had on him, but it is safe to say that Willy was deprived of the masculine influence which allowed Ben to so blithely head for Alaska and wind up in Africa. Furthermore, imagine Willy just wandering off, leaving Linda alone with Happy and Biff, as his father had left his mother alone with two sons. It is unthinkable in modern society. Willy accepts his father's and Ben's desertion as the mark of a man, but his sons, brought up in a different tradition, would not have so honored him had he followed his father's lead.

That the feminine influence continues to be dominant in Willy's life is made clear when Linda discourages him from accepting the one opportunity which would allow him to fulfill his pioneer yearnings. Linda, who is usually thought of as passive, quite actively frustrates the pioneer in Willy because she fears it. She represents the values of modern society, not the values Willy would be able to apply in Alaska:

> BEN. Now, look here, William. I've bought timberland in Alaska and I need a man to look after things for me.
> WILLY. God, timberland! Me and my boys in those grand outdoors (Act II, p. 183).

Ben needs a *man,* and this is, at heart, all that Willy has dreamed of being. Both Biff and Happy are wrong at the end of the play when the former says that Willy dreamed of being "number-one man" and the latter that Willy's dreams were all wrong. All Willy has ever wanted is to be a *man,* in the sense that he understands that word, a man as his father was; Ben offers him the opportunity to be that man. Willy also conceives of the frontier as purely a man's world; in his initial excitement, he gives no thought to Linda but thinks only of "me and my boys."

> BEN. You've got a new continent at your doorstep, William. Get out of these cities, they're full of talk and time payments and courts of law. Screw on your fists and you can fight for a fortune out there.
> WILLY. Yes, yes! Linda, Linda!
> LINDA. Oh, you're back?
> BEN. I haven't much time.
> WILLY. No, wait! Linda, he's got a proposition for me in Alaska.
> LINDA. But you've got—*To Ben:* He's got a beautiful job here.
> WILLY. But in Alaska, kid, I could—
> LINDA. You're doing well enough, Willy.
> BEN, *to Linda.* Enough for what, my dear?
> LINDA, *frightened of Ben and angry at him.* Don't say those things to him! Enough to be happy right here, right now. *To Willy while Ben laughs:* Why must everybody conquer the world? You're well liked, and the boys love you, and someday—*to Ben*—why, old man Wagner told him just the other day that if he keeps it up he'll be a member of the firm, didn't he, Willy? (Act II, pp. 183-84).

What Linda does not understand is that Willy was brought up in a tradition in which one had worlds to conquer and that the attempt to conquer them was the mark of a man. Hers is the voice that Ben refers to, the voice representative of the time payments which punctuate the play and become the dominant symbol of modern society. Even at Willy's death, Linda does not understand how little and yet, in this society, how much Willy really wanted. Charley, who throughout the play seems so insensitive to Willy's problems, understands, but Linda cannot:

> LINDA. I can't understand it. At this time especially. First time in thirty-five years we were just about free and clear. He only needed a little salary. He was even finished with the dentist.
> CHARLEY. No man only needs a little salary.
> LINDA. I can't understand it (Requiem, p. 221).

Indeed, in Linda's farewell to Willy, the time payment becomes an epitaph. Linda's parting words are doubly ironical if one thinks of Willy as frustrated pioneer—in modern society, the last payment on the house always comes too late, and a man, while he lives, is never free. One is obliged, at this point, to compare Willy with his father, whose house was a wagon on wheels which he owned utterly, and whose freedom was such that he could abandon this symbol of mobility and independence in search of an even greater freedom:

> LINDA. Forgive me, dear. I can't cry. I don't know what it is, but I can't cry. I don't understand it. Why did you ever do that? Help me, Willy, I can't cry. It seems to me that you're just on another trip. I keep expecting you. Willy, dear, I can't cry. Why did you do it? I search and search and I search, and I can't understand it, Willy. I made the last payment on the house today. Today, dear. And there'll be nobody home. . . . We're free and clear. . . . We're free. . . . We're free. . . . We're free. . .(Requiem, pp. 221-22).

Willy has succeeded in passing on his inherited values to his sons, but they are of as little value to Happy and Biff as they are to Willy. Indeed, their failures can be understood in terms of the same conflict between peddler and pioneer that ruins Willy. Quite simply, there is a good deal of the peddler in Happy, but there is also some of the pioneer in him, too, and the pioneer frustrates the peddler in him:

> HAPPY. Sometimes I want to just rip my clothes off in the middle of the store and outbox that goddam merchandise manager. I mean I can outbox, outrun, and outlift anybody in that store, and I have to take orders from those common, petty sons-of-bitches till I can't stand it any more (Act I, pp. 139-40).

The reverse is true of Biff: he is predominantly pioneer but there is enough peddler in him to frustrate the pioneer:

> BIFF. Hap, I've had twenty or thirty different kinds of jobs since I left home before the war, and it always turns out the same. I just realized it

lately. In Nebraska when I herded cattle, and the Dakotas, and Arizona, and now in Texas. It's why I came home now, I guess, because I realized it. This farm I work on, it's spring there now, see? And they've got about fifteen new colts. There's nothing more inspiring or—beautiful than the sight of a mare and a new colt. And it's cool there now, see? Texas is cool now, and it's spring. And whenever spring comes to where I am, I suddenly get the feeling, my God, I'm not getting anywhere! What the hell am I doing, playing around with horses, twenty-eight dollars a week! I'm thirty-four years old, I oughta be makin' my future. That's when I come running home. And now, I get here, and I don't know what to do with myself (Act I, pp. 138-39).

That the attempt to wed the peddler and pioneer is fatal is dramatized by Willy's suicide, for only in death can they be successfully combined. In committing suicide, Willy is still the peddler, selling his life for a profit, bartering his existence for a legacy for Biff; but he is also a pioneer, penetrating unknown and dangerous territory. Ben tells him, "It's dark there, but full of diamonds" (Act II, p. 219)—Africa-black, Alaska-white, one suspects.

In some way, Willy's death liberates both Biff and Happy in that it kills that frustrating element in each of them. Willy's death kills the pioneer in Happy, in whom the peddler has always dominated, forever:

HAPPY. I'm staying right here in this city, and I'm gonna beat this racket! . . . I'm gonna show you and everybody else that Willy Loman did not die in vain. He had a good dream. It's the only dream you can have—to come out number-one man. He fought it out here, and this is where I'm gonna win it for him (Requiem, p. 222).

And it kills the peddler in Biff: at the end of the play, Biff goes West, presumably for good. Biff's liberation is more positive because, by embracing the pioneer, he embraces that part of Willy he has always loved;

BIFF. There were a lot of nice days. When he'd come home from a trip; or on Sundays, making the stoop; finishing the cellar; putting on the new porch; when he built the extra bathroom; and put up the garage (Requiem, p. 221).

One immediately recalls Biff's statement in Act I, ". . . we don't belong in this nut-house of a city! We should be mixing cement on some open plain . . . ." (Act I, p. 166). However much the pioneer in Willy is stifled, it is the little expression he does give it—making repairs on the house—that guarantees him a small modicum of immortality:

BIFF. You know something, Charley, there's more of him in that front stoop than in all the sales he ever made (Requiem, p. 221).

Death of a Salesman, then, is, from one viewpoint, a search for identity, one man's attempt to be a man according to the frontier tradition in which he was raised and a failure to achieve that identity because in this time and in this place that identity cannot be achieved. That is what Biff means when he says, "He never knew who he was" (Requiem, p. 221). But it is also, in the end, a search for identity that succeeds, for Willy in death, but for Biff in life. And that is what Biff means when he says, "I know who I am, kid" (Requiem, p. 222).

John V. Hagopian

Arthur Miller: The *Salesman's* Two Cases

A careful study of *Death of a Salesman* in terms of Arthur Miller's own defense of it in various articles, prefaces, and interviews leads to the conclusion that the author himself does not understand his own accomplishment—and his confusion is shared by his critics. The fact of the matter is that not only is Miller's salesman suffering from schizophrenia, but the play itself is afflicted with that disease. Most plays, like most people, have multiple facets to their personalities, but these usually function more or less harmoniously within a single integrated being. The two personalities of Miller's play do, of course, interrelate, but they are basically different genres—a dazzlingly experimental social drama is the dominant personality, but it detracts our attention from the more important and more conventionally-made drama of a moral struggle toward insight and honest personal commitment.

Shortly after the premiere of *Death of a Salesman,* Arthur Miller defended his play in the *New York Times* from certain critical attacks by asserting that "the common man is as apt a subject for tragedy in its highest sense as the kings were. . . . The tragic feeling is evoked in us when we are in the presence of a character who is ready to lay down his life, if need be, to secure one thing—his sense of personal dignity."[1] He elaborated his arguments in the introduction to *A View from the Bridge,* where he said that all good drama is

Reprinted from *Modern Drama,* VI (September, 1963), 117-25, by permission of the journal and of A. C. Edwards.
[1] Quotations from critics and from Arthur Miller's remarks (except those from the Preface to his *Collected Plays*) are all taken from *Two Modern American Tragedies,* ed. by J. D. Hurrell (N.Y.: Scribner's, 1961).

essentially social drama, depicting man in a struggle to wrest from his society some recognition of his worth not as a customer, draftee, machine tender, ideologist, or whatever, but as a human being. Modern society refuses to grant him that recognition, and any determined effort to secure it is doomed to end tragically. "The reason *Death of a Salesman* . . . left such a strong impression was that it set forth unremittingly the picture of a man who was not even especially 'good' but whose situation made clear that at bottom we are alone, valueless, without even the elements of a human person, when once we fail to fit the patterns of [social] efficiency." The fullest discussion of the genesis, form, and meaning of all of Miller's plays to date is in his introduction to the *Collected Plays,*[2] where Miller takes his critics to task for misreading *Death of a Salesman* as an anticapitalistic play or as a document of futility and pessimism. Perhaps Miller's most significant comment is that "Willy Loman has broken a law [of modern culture just as Oedipus had of Greek culture] without whose protection life is unsupportable if not incomprehensible to him and to many others; it is the law which says that a failure in society and in business has no right to live. . . . My attempt in the play was to counter this [law] with an opposing system which, so to speak, is in a race for Willy's faith, and it is the system of love which is the opposite of the law of success. It is embodied in Biff Loman, but by the time Willy can perceive his love it can serve only as an ironic comment upon the life he sacrificed for power and for success and its tokens."

Obviously, Miller focuses his attention on Willy Loman—Biff functions in a subplot designed to serve merely as an "ironic comment" on the main plot. But intention does not here square with achievement. Miller and his critics are in error in seeing the central character of the play in Willy Loman. The protagonist of a drama must be the one who struggles most for understanding, who faces the most crucial question, who achieves the most transforming insight, and whose motives, decisions, and actions most influence the total situation. By these criteria the main figure of *Death of a Salesman* is not Willy, whose understanding and values change not one bit from the beginning to the end; it is Biff Loman, who is seeking to "find himself" and does so in making an anguished choice between clear-cut alternatives—continued drifting or redeeming himself, achieving vitality at the sacrifice of his father and his father's values. Willy is simply a man to whom things happen and who responds with bewilderment and a desperate clinging to his old faith; Biff is a man who ultimately makes things happen, who responds to the great trauma in his life first with an emotional and moral paralysis and then with a determined effort to face the truth at whatever cost.

Probably the chief reason why audiences and critics have difficulty seeing

---

[2] From this point on, all of Arthur Miller's remarks are taken from the Preface of his *Collected Plays* (N.Y.: Viking Press, 1957).

this pattern of dramatic meaning is that Miller has experimented in drama with the two major innovations of modern fiction: stream-of-consciousness, and the controlling intelligence of a limited point of view. Since both techniques are used to construct Willy Loman, the dramatic pyrotechnics illuminate the salesman out of all proportion to his real dramatic, philosophical, and psychological importance. "The first image that occurred to me," says Miller, "was of an enormous face the height of the proscenium arch which would appear and then open up, and we would see the inside of a man's head. In fact, *The Inside of His Head* was the first title. . . . I wished to create a form which . . . would literally be the process of Willy Loman's way of mind." Even without the physical image of the huge head, Miller has succeeded in making the action of the play largely the stream-of-consciousness of Willy; through fluid stage setting and bold use of lighting the memories and hallucinations of Willy are rendered not as "flashbacks" to earlier events objectively seen but as happenings of the present in Willy's mind. But Miller has paid the price of having audiences respond emotionally to the medium itself rather than see through it to the magnificent drama which it contains. For it seems that Miller has created *Death of a Salesman* with artistic intuition rather than critical intelligence, despite his *ex post facto* suggestions to the contrary. For example, he says, "What was wanted . . . was not a mounting line of tension, nor a gradually narrowing cone of intensifying suspense, but a bloc, a single chord presented as such at the outset . . . to hold back nothing . . . even at the cost of suspense and climax." To be sure, in so far as Willy is not merely the medium but the subject of the drama, Miller has almost achieved his aim despite the fact that drama is a temporal, dynamic medium which must move forward. The very first image of Willy is of a man utterly defeated—"I'm tired to the death. I couldn't make it. I just couldn't make it, Linda," he says. And his death at the end of the play is merely confirmation of the fact established at the outset. However, in so far as Willy's mind is the frame, the controlling intelligence, the stream-of-consciousness within which is enacted the drama of Biff, there is a beautifully structured line of mounting tension. To a large degree, the movement of the play is exactly like that of Sophocles's *Oedipus*; the drama moves forward by accumulating significant moments of the past that gradually illuminate the central problem—the conflict between the father and his oldest son. Exactly what is that conflict? What brought it about? How will it be resolved?—these are the questions that are involved in the central movement. And although everyone in the play at some point or other faces that problem, it is Biff who acts to resolve it.

The very first dialogue of the play sets it up:

WILLY. There's such an undercurrent in him. He became a moody man . . . .

LINDA. . . . I think if he finds himself, then you'll both be happier and not fight any more.

· / · · · · · · · · · ·

WILLY. Why did he come home? I would like to know what brought him home.

LINDA. I don't know. I think he's still lost, Willy. I think he's very lost.

Biff is indeed lost, and he has come home to make one final effort to resolve his inner conflict; but at this stage, of course, we still do not know what the conflict is about. The dialogue suggests that it somehow has to do with his relations with his father, a notion confirmed in Biff's first dialogue with Happy:

HAPPY. . . . What happened, Biff? Where's the old humor, the old confidence? (He shakes Biff's knee. Biff gets up and moves restlessly about the room.) What's the matter?

BIFF. Why does Dad mock me all the time? . . . / . . . Everything I say there's a twist of mockery on his face. I can't get near him.

· ·

HAPPY. I think the fact that you're not settled, that you're still kind of up in the air . . .

BIFF. There's one or two other things depressing him, Happy.

HAPPY. What do you mean?

BIFF. Never mind. Just don't lay it all to me.

No suspense? No mounting line of tension? Only the most insensitive member of the audience would not at this point feel a rising curiosity focussed specifically on Biff's problem with his father. In the ensuing dialogue, Biff recapitulates his misery in trying to establish a foothold in the business world after leaving high school and the contrasting peace and content he experienced while working on a ranch in Texas: "There's nothing more inspiring or—beautiful than the sight of a mare and a new colt," an effective symbol of his urge toward vitality and creativity. Then why, as Willy had asked earlier, has he come home? Because his family is the arena of his unresolved conflict. Biff then listens in amazement and despair to his father's hallucinatory recapitulation of the idyllic past when he was still the idolized god of his sons, inculcating in them the false values he persisted in holding despite the fact that they did not work for him. That long scene ends with a revelation of Willy's immense feeling of guilt concerning his philandering during his lonely and unsuccessful treks to the markets of New England. No specific connection is made between that guilt and the father-son conflict, but again and again the first act thrusts relentlessly toward illumination of the conflict and an implicit connection is made.

When the neighbor, Charley (the chorus figure of the play), comes over to calm Willy after his raving hallucination, Willy says, "I can't understand it. He's going back to Texas again. . . . I got nothin' to give him, Charley;" and his kindly neighbor advises him to forget it, to release the boy, to let him live his own life according to his own code. Then, after Charley leaves and Willy decides to go for a walk, the two sons come down to discuss their father's plight with their mother and again the father-son issue is faced:

> LINDA. When you write you're coming, he's all smiles. . . . And then the closer you come, the more shaky he gets. . . . He can't bring himself to open up to you. Why are you so hateful to each other? Why is that?

Biff is evasive and conciliatory, but the mother insists that the sons must have respect for their father, be concerned about his distraught and pitiable condition—"What happened to the love you had for him?"

> BIFF. . . . I know he's a fake and he doesn't like anybody around who knows!
> LINDA. Why a fake? In what way? What do you mean?
> BIFF. Just don't lay it all at my feet. It's between me and him—that's all I have to say.

Again, the revelation of the cause of the conflict is avoided, but it is foreshadowed when Linda, describing Willy's attempts at suicide, refers to a woman and Biff sharply interrupts with a tense question, "What woman?" before Linda can explain that she is referring to a woman who had witnessed Willy's deliberate smash-up in his car. Finally, this powerful dramatic line culminates at the end of the first act in a tremendous confrontation scene between father and son. The clash between their *social* values, which has been clear since the opening dialogue between Biff and Happy, is now openly faced, but the more powerful cause of discord, the *private,* secret anguish caused by the awareness of both father and son that Willy has betrayed the love of his family, is only darkly suggested:

> BIFF. . . . They've laughed at Dad for years, and you know why? Because we don't belong in this nuthouse of a city! We should be mixing cement on some open plain, or—or carpenters . . .
> . . . .
> WILLY. Why do you always insult me?
> . . . .
> BIFF. Oh, Jesus, I'm going to sleep!
> WILLY. Don't curse in this house!
> BIFF. Since when did you get so clean?

But Biff succumbs to the forces of family reconciliation and reluctantly agrees to make an attempt to fulfill his father's dream for him. However, the first act ends ominously with Biff in the cellar holding the rubber tubing with which Willy has been planning to commit suicide, while Linda timidly asks the key question of the play: "Willy, dear, what has he got against you?"

Act II opens late the following morning with Willy announcing that he has "slept like a dead one" but feeling very optimistic. But the catastrophes begin to mount when, symbolically foreshadowing the climax of the play, the son of Willy's former boss (also his own godson) dismisses Willy from his job. In desperation Willy calls upon Charley to borrow money for the payment of his insurance premium, and in Charley's office the key question is again posed by Bernard, but this time much more narrowly focussed in time and place:

> WILLY. ... There's something I don't understand. ... His life ended after that Ebbets Field game. From the age of seventeen nothing good ever happened to him ... / ... Why did he lay down?
> BERNARD. ... I got the idea he'd gone up to New England to see you. Did he have a talk with you then? ... / ... When he came back. ... I knew he'd given up his life. What happened in Boston, Willy?

Willy is unable to face that question. At the restaurant where the victory banquet turns into a shambles when it is revealed that not only has Willy lost his job but that Biff was unable to get one, Willy interrupts Biff's attempts to explain with the outburst: "I'm not interested in stories about the past." However, as inexorably as in Sophocles, the past must be faced. It rises in Willy's fantasies and collides head-on with the present that it has led to. As in Freudian psychotherapy, well-being can be restored only when the suppressed traumas of the past can be raised to consciousness and abreacted. The penultimate crisis of the play (and the answer to the intensely persistent question raised in the beginning: "What happened, Biff?") is reached when through Willy's consciousness we see enacted the shocking confrontation of the penitent son and the philandering father in a Boston hotel room fifteen years earlier. Biff's idol is shattered: "You fake! You phony little fake! You fake!" It is this discovery that had poisoned their relations and had rendered Biff unable to reconcile himself to his father's values. But neither had he the strength to reject his father, for that would mean cutting himself off from the strongest source of love he had ever known.

Now we are ready for the ambivalence to be resolved, and the final crisis occurs when Willy and Biff meet at home that evening. Biff announces to his mother "with absolute assurance, determination: 'We're gonna have an abrupt conversation, him and me.' " Biff does not intend to expose his father, as Willy fears, but he has resolved to break with him, to declare his independence, to assert his own identity and his own values: "I'm saying good-by to you, Pop . . . / . . . Today I realized something about myself. . . . To hell with whose fault it is or anything like that. Let's just wrap it up, heh?" But Willy cannot believe that rejection without hatred is possible and he provokes a scene that for emotional tension and dramatic illumination is one of the finest in modern drama. The discovery of the self and the honest assertion of it regardless of the consequences has always been the high point of the greatest tragedies. Here it has tragic consequence, but not for the protagonist; hence, *Death of a Salesman* is, in the highest sense as explained by Susanne Langer, a comedy. Because the forces that obstruct the development of vitality are grappled with and overthrown.

This fact is lost in the elaborate dramatic frame, Willy's consciousness, which calls excess attention to itself. The powerfully dynamic story of Biff is obscured and almost lost in the tidal waves of tragic feeling that wash over it. That is perhaps why there is so much critical controversy over whether or not *Death of a Salesman* is a tragedy. Even with Willy as protagonist, despite the immense pathos of his experience, there is a legitimate question. To be sure, *Hamlet, Samson Agonistes,* and other tragedies do open with the central characters already in a posture of defeat, but they at least achieve some insight and face their deaths with some degree of understanding. Willy Loman goes to his death still blindly committed to his false ideals. The fact that he does so out of an overwhelming love for his son and gratitude for the return of his son's love makes his gesture deeply pathetic, but hardly tragic. Within this frame of pathos is the experience of Biff in which we see an action that is serious, complete, and of sufficient magnitude, including a dynamic plot with ascending crises, epiphany, peripeteia, ethos, and dianoia. Arthur Miller himself has been so preoccupied with his pathetic salesman that he does not realize that his own play does contain ethos (the moral decisions of a character) and dianoia (the ability of a character to say what is fitting in a given situation); he claims that *"Death of a Salesman* is a slippery play to categorize because nobody in it stops to make a speech objectively stating the great issues which I believe it embodies." What, then, are we to make of Biff's climactic speech which reveals that he has gained insight into himself, that he understands the issues involved in the conflict, and that he has made the morally and psychologically right decision?

> BIFF. No! Nobody's hanging himself, Willy! I ran down eleven flights with a pen in my hand today. And suddenly I stopped, you hear me? And in the middle of that office building, do you hear this? I stopped in the middle of that building and I saw—the sky. I saw the things that I love in this world. The work and the food and time to sit and smoke. And I looked at the pen and said to myself, what the hell am I grabbing this for? Why am I trying to become what I don't want to be? What am I doing in an office, making a contemptuous, begging fool of myself, when all I want is out there, waiting for me the minute I say I know who I am!

In his desperate fury to make his father understand, Biff seems on the verge of attacking him, but he breaks down sobbing, pleading for release from his father's phony dream. Willy, wild with relief at discovering that his son, far from hating him, truly loves him in spite of everything, relapses into his old dream: "That boy—that boy is going to be magnificent! ... / ... Can you imagine that magnificence with twenty thousand dollars in his pocket?" He rushes off to commit suicide, certain that with the insurance money Biff will "be ahead of Bernard again." But the dialogue of the "Requiem" shows that Biff is a new man, that he—and only he—truly understood his father: "He had the wrong dreams. All, all wrong ... / ... He never knew who he was ... / ... I know who I am."

There is, then, in *Death of a Salesman* a play within the play. Perhaps in the pre-Freudian era it was not possible for a drama to show a son resolving his Oedipus Complex by consigning his father to death without experiencing such tremendous guilt that the only possible consequence was tragedy. In Arthur Miller's play the son breaks away from the father image and in effect consigns him to death *without* the tragic consequences. However, for reasons impossible to determine here, Miller did not focus on that action, but rather on the pitiable father's fate. The result is a curious dramatic astigmatism.

The drama of Willy, daringly experimental in technique, has properly been described as social criticism; Harold Clurman calls it "a challenge to the American dream. ... The death of Miller's salesman is symbolic of the breakdown of the whole concept of salesmanship inherent in our society." But Arthur Miller has denied that it is an anticapitalistic play. "A play," he says, "cannot be equated with a political philosophy ... / ... provided, of course, that it is a play, which is to say a work of art." He says further, "The most decent man in *Death of a Salesman* is a capitalist (Charley) whose aims are not different from Willy Loman's. The great difference between them is that Charley is not a fanatic." Again, it must be concluded that Arthur Miller does not understand his own play. For one thing Charley's aims *regarding his son* are manifestly different from Willy's, but even on the socio-economic level Miller's remarks are misleading. To be sure, in its larger dimensions *Death of a Salesman* is not *primarily* concerned with politics or economics. Nevertheless, to the extent that it is concerned with these problems the play is clearly an indictment of the profit motive, of competitive salesmanship, and of planned obsolescence—three principal features of capitalistic society that distinguish it from other socio-economic systems. When Willy is cruelly deprived of his job after some forty years with the firm, Howard explains, "It's a business, kid, and everybody's gotta pull his own weight. ... Business is business." And Willy howls in protest against planned obsolescence: "Once in my life I would like to own something outright before it's broken! I'm always in a race with the junkyard! I just finished paying for the car and it's on its last legs. The refrigerator consumes belts like a maniac. They time those things. They time them so when you finally paid for them, they're used up."

Miller has said also that the exponents of socialism cannot take heart from his work because "there is no such thing as a capitalist assembly line or drygoods counter. . . . So long as modern man conceives of himself as valuable only because he fits into some niche in the machine-tending pattern, he will never know anything more than a pathetic doom." There is truth in this, and *Death of a Salesman* is broadly an indictment of all modern industrial society; nevertheless, in specifically attacking the profit motive, competitive salesmanship, and planned obsolescence, this play does specifically isolate the capitalistic form of modern society as its target.

This social problem drama of Willy Loman exists mainly in the outer frame of the play. In technique the inner drama is successfully integrated with the frame, but it is not so successfully integrated in content. That inner drama—Biff's drama—quite traditional in form and technique, has not been sufficiently appreciated as a uniquely American manifestation of the eternal, humanizing struggle of a man to achieve his own identity, even if it means the sacrifice of those he loves.

3. As Tragedy

Remy G. Saisselin

Is Tragic Drama Possible in the Twentieth Century?

The question is not whether tragedy or a tragic experience are possible, but the tragic drama. We assume then that we are dealing with a literary genre and base our arguments on the analysis of works which have traditionally been held to be tragedies; on the assumption that there is a link between tragic drama and society, between this type of drama and a certain concept of man and of human destiny.

All this is not explicitly stated in the first and perhaps most lucid of all treatises on tragedy, the *Poetics* of Aristotle, but it is implied. Tragedy as a genre presupposes that a certain society assumes what has come to be called the tragic vision of life, assumes that man is free, has a conscience, sins through pride, is punished for it, that consequently the universe is not always a very hospitable place for man, and finally that the victim of a tragic experience be conscious of it and its implications.[1]

But tragedy also supposes an aristocratic society and values, that is value put on reason, conscience, grandeur; for it will be observed that the tragic hero is ever a noble man. He is also a universal man and this in turn presupposes, on the part of the dramatist, generosity, for if the noble man is to be the universal man, then man in general is well thought of.

At the same time tragedy is the tale of the failure of the noble man: "Tragedy shows us a moral will engaged in an unequal struggle with destiny, whether that destiny be represented by the forces within or without the mind."[2] And the commentator goes on to point out that ". . . in tragedy those are doomed who innocently err no less than those who sin consciously. Nay, the tragic irony sometimes lies precisely herein, that owing to some inherent frailty or flaw—it may be human shortsightedness, it may be some error of blood or judgment—the very virtues of man hurry him forward to his ruin."[3] But if tragedy be the tale of failure, it is nevertheless that of a noble failure, a redeeming defeat from which the victim emerges triumphant so that

Reprinted from *The Theatre Annual,* XVII (1960), 12-21, by permission of the journal and of John V. Falconieri.

[1]On the question of freedom and responsibility, see William G. McCollom, *Tragedy* (N.Y., 1957): "The tragic character is a conscious agent. He is also free. If he were not, tragedy could not be a moral action in any meaningful sense of that expression. But tragedy is a monument to the freedom of human choice" (p. 26).

[2]See *Aristotle's Theory of Fine Art,* tr. and with an introduction and critical notes by S. H. Butcher (Dover Publications, 1951), p. 311.

[3]*Ibid.,* pp. 321-22.

tragedy becomes, in a certain sense, a commentary upon the injustice of the gods and the universe.

Thus man emerges triumphant even in defeat, a triumph emphasized by lucidity and the conscience of suffering. Oedipus, Macbeth, Othello, Hamlet are greatest in their moments of lucidity when the truth of their error is borne upon them. So too with the characters of Racine who in their certain, continuous, and merciless loss of hope, watch themselves be pulled towards final defeat. Thus may we compare the tragic hero to Pascal's thinking reed: "Man is but a reed, the feeblest thing in nature; but he is a thinking reed. The whole of the universe need not arm itself to crush him; a vapor, a drop of water, suffice to kill him. But though the entire universe were to crush him, man would still be nobler than that which destroys him, for he knows he is dying, whereas the universe knows nothing of the advantage it has over him." And thus did Phèdre come to know her fate and deplore it:

> Ce n'est plus une ardeur dans mes veines cachée:
> C'est Vénus toute entière à sa proie attachée.

She suffers through her fate, combats it, succumbs to it, and becomes great in the conscience she has of her suffering. Athalie is sublime in much the same way when she admits her defeat in her cry:

> Dieu des Juifs, tu l'emportes!

Tragedy thus implies lucidity, or consciousness, suffering, a feeling of destiny on the supernatural plane, as was the case mostly in Greek tragedy, or on the human plane as is most often the case in Shakespearian or French tragedy, and in some dramas of Calderon. But always, one must be conscious of one's fate. In the words of Julien Benda: "Dramas of the conscious, true dramas of man. Those of the unconscious, Oh Romantics, he shares with the beasts, with the stones."[4] It seems to us that it is precisely this emphasis on the conscious which implies a value put on mind, on reason, for after all it is here that the Ancients sought the main distinction between man and beast.

Now one may well argue that tragic experience, or tragic events, are still possible in our day. This may well be, just as it may well be that a tragic character is still possible today. But the question is: do we still hold the tragic man up to admiration? Is the tragic stage still the mirror of society? We touch here upon the important question of the relation of tragedy, as a genre, to society.

---

[4] Julien Benda, *Délice d'Eleuthère* (Paris, 1935), p. 75.

It is well-known that Greek tragedy was linked with certain religious be-liefs.[5] It is not our intention to enter into this question here; it is not neces-sary to return to the Greeks to establish that our values and our way of living are foreign to that associated with the tragic vision. We shall merely go back to the seventeenth century. Aside from the fact that we are dealing, in the seventeenth century, with an aristocratic society, we immediately note too that the world-view pervading all the facets of life of the society that mat-tered at the time, was dramatic. Is there need to quote Macbeth? The world was a stage upon which men performed, played a role, and what mattered was that one play it well. And depending upon the role you aimed at you risked either tragedy or comedy. The system of values whereby a man's play was judged was inherited from Antiquity, modified by Christianity, and cherished by the nobility, or let us say an élite, which set the tone of what was an otherwise Christian society. We stress that we are dealing with a society which in one of its aspects is not Christian: moralists did not cease to point out that the values of the gentleman, the noble man of the period, were not Christian. Saint-Evremond, an epicurean of the period, went so far as to write that "The spirit of our religion is directly opposed to that of tragedy." Michel Butor has recently argued that one of the reasons Racine had to cease writing was because one could detect in his tragedies a hatred of the gods quite incom-patible with the Christian values officially held by the France of Louis XIV.[6] One might thus say that in the seventeenth century, tragedy was already, in a certain sense, out of place; especially if Greek tragedy is taken as a model.

For indeed Christianity offers a way out of tragedy. Yet it is not the only way of avoiding it. Tragedy can be read as a lesson and in one way we may say that the Stoics and Epicureans read it as such and acted upon their reading. For if tragedy is the result of ambition, pride, lack of measure; then withdrawal, the acceptance of one's limitations, become a means of avoiding tragedy.[7] The exercise of the will can be directed against the passions and you can retire into a garden with Epicurus or you can direct your mind to bow to the order of things with Epictetus. If you chose Christ, then destiny is re-placed by Providence and human sinfulness is redeemed by the suffering Christ. In all instances we are concerned with the human will, with human liberty, and all three sects teach a form of wisdom which avoids tragedy.

The modern world has rejected all these forms of wisdom; they are indeed no longer necessary because there is no need to avoid tragedy because we

---

[5]For an excellent essay on Greek tragedy see: M. Fernagu, "Le Tragique Grec," *Revue d'Esthetique*, XIII (Mars, 1960), 58-75.

[6] See the interesting essay by Michel Butor, "Racine et les dieux," in *Répertoire* (Paris, 1960).

[7]Fernagu, *op. cit.:* "Celui qui reste à l'intérieur des limites ne risque pas l'aventure tragique: le destin ne vient pas le chercher dans sa sagesse, voire dans sa médiocrité."

have replaced the tragic vision with something else which makes tragedy as a genre so difficult for the modern playwright.

In considering our vision of human destiny we must not forget that between us and the Elizabethans, not to say the Greeks, there stands the work left us by the Enlightenment and the nineteenth century. And since then we have all more or less been "Americanized." In the words of Count Calovoglio, that most civilized gentleman and hellenist of Norman Douglas's *South Wind,* we have come to substitute progress for civilization. We do not really believe in failure and our view of man is an optimistic one, in spite of the present fashion in modern literature and modern art to take a dim view of man and write "failure stories." The lack of generosity on the part of writers, which Mauriac so well referred to once as the "excrementalists," may point out certain evils, but it does not imply a return to the tragic vision of life associated with the tragic drama.[8] Indeed the dim view of man makes tragedy impossible. Furthermore, the writers of our time are not representative of the values of society, they are representative of their comments upon these values, and the separation of artist, writer, and public, too well known to need comment here. Our moderns, however, can hardly be blamed for their dim view of man.

For, having posed the idea of progress, and having accepted the belief in the perfectibility of man, we have come to found as the universal man, not the noble man, but the useful man, or the successful man, with success being measured in terms not of victory over the self, serenity, and wisdom attained, but utility to society, contributions to progress, and leisure spent in fishing and golf. And so we care no more for the great or noble man, not even for the man willing to die for what he believes in. We need not be deceived by the medals given to military heroes, the latter being the first to say that anyone could have done the same thing. And we know this to be true. We have seen too many heroes and we have seen them at too close a range.

To be sure the demolition of the hero, which is one aspect of the degradation of man, began long before our time, already in the seventeenth century with the critique of man by the Christian moralists.[9] To this degradation of man the Enlightenment added more weight. It is not for nothing that Voltaire should have written that he valued men who contribute to civilization more than mere heroes glorious on the battlefield. It is not for nothing that the eighteenth century brought forth no good tragedies and that the century saw the introduction of a new type of drama, the domestic tragedy based on the

---

[8] On the failure story see Thomas Munro, "The Failure Story: A Study of Contemporary Pessimism," *JAAC,* XVII (Dec., 1958 & Mar., 1959), 143-68, 362-87.

[9] See Paul Bénichou, *Morales du Grand Siècle* (Paris, 1948), passim.

common man, in a common situation, with common interests, and meant to
wring sentimental tears from the audience. But if we look further into the
assumptions held by the formers of public opinion at the time, we shall see
something even more interesting as regards the decline of the tragic genre,
namely the use of the stage as a lay pulpit. In the words of Mercier, an
Encyclopedist: "Theatre is made . . . to supplement youth's lack of experience, rectify the vision of those who have not seen well, help the intelligence
of mediocre minds, teach men, who sometimes are uncertain in their minds,
what they must hate, love, and esteem."[10] Now if Mercier writes as he does,
and many others along with him in the eighteenth century, if he means to use
the stage as a means of propagating the truth, it is because all the values
which had been generally held and accepted by society until the eighteenth
century, and which were the values which made tragedy as a genre possible,
were now in decline. The dramatist was thus no longer to be a mere commentator upon human destiny, he was to become a prophet announcing a
new truth, that of progress based upon the perfectibility of man, which term
is the very antithesis of the idea of man and human destiny implied in the
very term tragedy.

The Enlightenment thus not only eliminated the concept of sin as held in
the Christian outlook, it also eliminated the tragic flaw. The philosophy of
the Enlightenment thus goes beyond the Christian as well as the Antique
worlds. Both the wisdom of Antiquity and that of Christ are replaced by
knowledge translated into power. Evil disappears from history; it is merely
written off as lack of Enlightenment and education, which negative quality
cannot be corrected since a proper method for insuring progress and enlightenment has been found in reason and experimental science. Thus the drama
becomes possible, a moralizing play concerned with the right way of doing
certain things and the proper way of behavior to hold for the good of society.
The philosophy of the Enlightenment succeeded in simplifying the universe,
but at the expense of certain ancient insights into the nature of man.

One might suppose that the failure of the French Revolution, the series of
disastrous wars in our times, should have altered our optimism radically. It
has not, for we have not ceased to think of our destiny in terms of production and consumption. Furthermore, we have lost the ability to view man at a
generous distance. Racine knew very well that tragedy as a genre can only be
possible in terms of a certain perspective; the tragic hero must be viewed at a
distance: "Tragic characters," he wrote in his preface to *Bajazet,* a play the
action of which was not long removed in time from his contemporaries, but
set in the Ottoman Empire, thus removed in space, "must be looked at with
an eye other than the one we ordinarily use to look at people we have seen
close to us. One may say that the respect we have for the heroes increases

---

[10]*Du Théâtre, ou Nouvel essai sur l'art dramatique* (Amsterdam, 1773), pp. 15-16.

with the distance they remove themselves from us: *Major e longinguo reverentia."* Not only have we unlearned this, but we have come to pry into what were once considered the innermost secrets of man. This may be medically desirable and justified, but it makes for bad theater and poor literature. It makes for case studies, but not tragedies. Oedipus may have given his name to a particular type of case, but the *Oedipus Rex* is not a case study.

However, this progressive degradation of man, and I use this term in an almost military way, in the sense of reducing to the ranks, this degradation does not mean that there are no tragic characters left in our day. One may think of Wilson as such; one may envisage Pourtalès, German Ambassador to Russia in 1914, and weeping upon the shoulder of Sazanoff at the end of the July crisis of that year, as a tragic character in a tragic situation and highly aware of it; one may even think of the Roosevelt of 1941 in those terms. However, we are so used to looking at men and events in the manner the historians have taught us, that is, objectively, or scientifically, or at least what passes as such, that we are no longer capable of making drama out of such situations. We are too used to thinking in terms of complex political, social, and economic situations and forces and trends. True, we may see men as victims of forces created by themselves, gotten beyond their control, and destroying them, but this, as we shall see, implies not tragedy, but the drama of the absurd. In passing, since this problem bears upon a peculiar vision of, and writing, of history, let us note that Tocqueville has pointed out that it is in democratic societies, those which were the result of the philosophy of the Enlightenment, that historians tend to write of events as the result of impersonal forces, while in aristocratic societies one views them as the result of the will of single men. Thus Shakespeare could still reasonably write a tragedy of Ceasar and not make of it unreasonable history for humanist historiography: Ceasar was ambitious! this can be understood by the Ancients as well as by the Elizabethans. But today we might rather think in terms of entrenched reactionary interests. This might be historically accurate and defensible, but it makes for bad theater. We have done too much research to write tragedies or even humanistic histories.

What then do we see? And what is the vision of those who have come to perceive the vanity of the philosophy of progress? Have they, as Camus argued they should, opted for the *pensée de midi,* the Greek vision? Not so, they have not gone beyond the absurd, which in fact represents not only a post-tragic vision, but also a post-progress vision and corresponding type of dramatic action.

Anouilh's *Antigone* is of importance in considering this new type of drama. The most sympathetic character here is not so much Antigone herself as her uncle Creon, and he comes closest to being a tragic character. But he is not one, and neither is Antigone. In fact he represents a point of view which is beyond tragedy, as well as being beyond Christ, Epicurus, or Marcus Aurelius; his view is beyond the idea of progress too. Antigone's symbolic burial of her brother is of no metaphysical consequence in the play. She herself knows that it is meaningless and absurd, just as she knows her brothers were good-for-nothings, *des vauriens.*[11] The gods are long since dead and with them fate. Creon is not a man who defies the universe and he has even ceased to be ambitious. Indeed, why be ambitious in an absurd universe? He merely does his task and exercises his *métier de roi* for reasons which have nothing to do with grandeur, glory, or power. To lead his people is a task which someone has to do and like Hoederer in Sartre's *Dirty Hands,* he accepts the necessity of dirtying his hands, and these, unlike those of Macbeth, no longer concern his conscience. Creon is the closest an administrator can get to being tragic. There is neither nobility nor heroism involved here: "They say it is a dirty job, but if it is not done, who will do it?" Creon is post-Enlightenment man, stripped of the illusion of the perfectibility of man. His values are those of the bourgeoisie, but a bourgeoisie unsure of its rights; as he explains to Antigone: "You too will learn, too late, that life is a book you love, a child at your feet, a tool in you hand, a bench to rest on in the evening in front of your house. You'll despise me for this, but you'll see that to discover this is the derisory consolation of growing old: perhaps, after all, life is only happiness." This is the wisdom not only of a retired *grand fonctionnaire,* but also of an aging man. There is toughness in it, and also a certain melancholy, which makes Creon admirable if not sublime. But it does not make him a tragic character. He governs a society which has solved the problem of tragedy so that if you would have tragedy, you must go out of your way to seek it, and doing this you are not a tragic character in the classic sense of the term, for then tragedy was visited upon you, though you might provoke it, but rather you become a latter-day version of the romantic hero in a society which is no longer amused by romantic antics.

Thus Antigone creates her own tragedy, willingly, arbitrarily. She is not the victim of fate, either of one outside herself, or one within herself, such as that which destroys her brothers in Racine's version of the same play, *La Thébaïde.* One might say that she wills herself to death the instant she refuses the lessons which can be drawn from tragedy, namely wisdom, and understanding: "Moi, je ne veux pas comprendre." Had she accepted understanding, then she could have lived. But she does not want to be bourgeois and so brands herself as an *entêtée* rather than a tragic figure, and her "tragedy" is perhaps that of an adolescent refusing to grow up. But

---

[11] On the difference between Anouilh and Sophocles, see the suggestive essay by Enrique Anderson Imbert, "Antigona: De Sofocles a Anouilh," in *Los Grandes Libros de Occidente* (Mexico, 1957).

tragedy, that of the Greeks, Elizabethans, and the French classics, was that of mature men and women.

Now if Anouilh's *Antigone* indicates why tragedy might not be possible in our times in Europe, Miller's *The Death of a Salesman* shows us why it is hardly possible in the United States.[12] This is like saying that Miller shows us why tragedy is not possible in the eighteenth century, for the values of our society are essentially those of a successful Enlightenment philosophy. The philosophy of the absurd, so widespread among men of letters in Europe, points out that Europe, as represented by its *littérateurs* and philosophers, has come to see that the values were false from the start. Willy Loman has not. He is not an absurd man; he is merely pathetic: he is neither tough, as is Creon, nor does he even possess the latter's bourgeois wisdom, a wisdom much scoffed at on the left bank, but sadly lacking on this side of the Atlantic. And so the Salesman is a man who dies having learned nothing. To be sure he is in the very heart of our society, representative of it as the tragic characters had to be representative of their society, but he is not of universal interest and he is not noble. One might thus define the *Death of a Salesman* as a *pathétie* whereas the dramas of Anouilh, Sartre, Camus may be thought of as "tragedy on the edge of society," much closer to the romantic drama than classical tragedy, for we are dealing with people who, much like the romantics, go out of their way to seek out adventure. Wisdom is rejected, but one does not for that find oneself in the situation existing previous to tragedy, one finds oneself in the midst of the absurd, a world of meaningless and gratuitous acts: it is as if Macbeth were to start his action after his pronouncement to the effect men's acts signify nothing.

Thus we live in a world in which tragic events and tragic persons, in real life, are still very much possible. But such events and persons are looked upon as exceptions by mankind at large, which part still views the condition of man in terms of a diluted and much vulgarized philosophy of the Enlightenment. The isolation of the artist and the writer may make for a drama of the absurd, but can it make for tragedy?

---

[12]Professor McCollom puts it as follows: "Although *Death of a Salesman* moves its audience, it fails as tragedy because Miller fails to see that the world of tragedy must be more than a temporary political and social climate if the hero is to have more than a transitory significance" (p. 17).

George de Schweinitz

Death of a Salesman:
A Note on Epic and Tragedy

For more than ten years Arthur Miller's *Death of a Salesman* has stirred up controversy. Is it really the tragedy its author so eloquently claims it to be?[1] One way of answering this question is to find some defining measures in the tragic tradition of Western culture and apply them to the play.

A glance back at Western literature shows immediately that tragedy and epic are often intermixed: witness *Paradise Lost* and *Moby-Dick*. In the epic, traditional value structures are probed and explored, perhaps recreated; in the tragedy, collisions between "units" in these structures precipitate catastrophe. The fundamental concern for such structures in both forms makes an intimate, and perhaps indissoluble, tie between tragedy and epic.

Besides being thus related, the epic and tragedy seem to have further characteristics in common: both seem to require a certain richness or maturity in homogeneous living in the society from which they come and both seem to reveal this characteristic by laying, or containing, a ground-plan for that culture. Though ostensibly portraits of the culture of one people or nation, they are, in fact, portraits of the projection of that people's or nation's culture, including, of course, its values, upon the whole universe. For as a man rises to epic or tragic heights, his view does not stop at the borders of his own native land.

One further characteristic common to epic and tragedy is that the protagonist in both must be accorded an unremitting respect as representative of the general type man. It is precisely here that the question concerning Willy Loman as such a protagonist has chiefly centered. Given the character he has, can he thus represent the general type man? I think he can and does, just as I think Ahab could and did, and in the remainder of the paper I shall consider why.

A generally three-part division of value characterized the Western epic and tragedy against which I am measuring *Death of a Salesman.* This division was objectified in a similarly three-part division of the universe in which it was contained. The gods (or God) ruled above; man occupied the earth, conceived of as a kind of "middle ground," and below was the Underworld or Hell. The

Reprinted from *The Western Humanities Review, XIV* (Winter, 1960), 91-96, by permission of the journal and the author.

[1] Arthur Miller, "Tragedy and the Common Man," *Theatre Arts* (March, 1951), pp. 48 ff.; *Arthur Miller's Collected Plays* (New York, 1957), the playwright's introduction, pp. 22-40 especially but *passim*; and "The Family in Modern Drama," *The Atlantic Monthly* (April, 1956), pp. 35-41.

realm of value corresponding to these divisions were, of course, first, the "divine" and the "human." On an equally simple basis, the realm of value of the Underworld or Hell corresponded to the corruption or negation of either or both of the other realms and thus to a condition of "no-value."

The focal questions about *Death of a Salesman* then are: is there here a structure of value in any way analogous to that of the older epic and tragic tradition (this does not mean: are the values the same?)? And, if so, does it receive objectification in anything like the way in which such structures did in the older tradition? In other words, in *Death of a Salesman* are there spatial or geographical equivalents for the basic divisions of value whose collisions produce the tragedy?

To answer these crucial questions, we must first recognize what in American history and tradition adhered to or deviated from this principally Old World structure. In *Moby-Dick* the tragedy was the outgrowth both of traumatic conditions in the protagonist and crises in his society. The combination of the two was both the story of a heroic rebel against the blind strokes of an impersonal and indifferent fate (the tragic part) and the story of "worlds" adrift in a universe whose age-old compartments of value were coming apart at the seams (the epic part). It was a case of individual trauma ruthlessly exploiting social and cultural crises and social and cultural crises mercilessly, yet unavoidably, aggravating individual trauma. One played into the other and there was no final separation of one from the other.

Let us say that by the middle of the twentieth century there was almost nothing left of this original value structure. By that time, in America, if a man found a stable and reliable value structure, it would almost certainly have to be something that he forged himself. Culturally, there were three main sources for his values: American history and tradition, which a man might or might not know enough to make use of; the frontier, which by the beginning of the twentieth century had largely become fantasized and associated with a folklore by which the citizen rationalized and covered over his naked drives for power and "success" (among the frontier's legacies was the political and social catchword "rugged individualism"); and the city, a complex reality which, while not exactly new in history, had achieved so dominant a place in the totality of twentieth century American experience that it constituted a third and final main source of value.

It will be seen at once that Arthur Miller takes for granted in this play that the individual's achieving a stable and reliable value structure in America is purely an empirical process. Such a structure is not something already formed—say, like Catholicism—into which the individual fits; rather, it is something he develops out of the crucible of his own highly heterogeneous experience. As Miller says himself, he is not writing in and of an age of faith, but in and of an age of secularism. The differences between these two types of culture to Miller is reflected in the fact that religious feeling, as normally understood, has absolutely no place in his play. In it God's name is mentioned only in vain.

This means that the "top" level of the traditional epic and tragic division is empty. There is nobody or no group "up there." From "there," at least, there is no dispensing of perfect justice or eternal damnation. Willy, Biff, Linda, Howard, Charley, and Happy pay it no heed; and neither does anybody, apparently, in their world. Whereas Ahab made a great commotion about turning the traditionally "top" level upside down, as it were, and becoming the "high" priest of the negation of the traditional "highest," for Willy and his world there is not even any question of protest because these things simply have no reality for him. If you had whispered in Willy's ear, in his mad and culturally dictated race for sales:

> As flies to wanton boys, are we to the gods
> They kill us for their sport.

you would have stopped him dead in his tracks—for a moment. What gods?

Willy's universe, then, is a drastically reduced one, compared even to Ahab's. But though for him a traditional "divine" has been so unequivocally removed, there must be something in its place—a "top" of some kind must still remain—or there would be no conflict, tragic or otherwise. We are now left with two realms of our original three: the "human," corresponding to earth in the old systemization, and the realm of "no-value," corresponding to the Underworld or Hell. Between these two we must find the "higher" and "lower" in value which form the poles between which a tragic protagonist is stretched. The "heaven" or "abode of the gods" of tradition is now to be found somewhere on earth, presumably somewhere within the territorial boundaries of the United States, maybe, in the form of an idea, hovering over, if never entering, the head of our hero Willy. The "hell" of tradition is, of course, as always, right beside it, ready to negate it or any lesser value, since "hell" is traditionally and unchangeably the negation of all value.

At this point it will be necessary to turn back to the three main sources of value that the play posits as possible for—to use Miller's word—the "average" American of this age, that is, for the American who, like Willy, has what Miller calls "the common materials of life" to work with. American history and tradition is the first of these, the frontier the second, and the city the third and last.

Each of these three main sources of value is clearly objectified or particularized in *Death of a Salesman;* that is, each is given a "vehicle" or correlative in the total action and each shares objectively—or Realistically, to use Miller's term for this Ibsen-derived type of drama—in the total conflict leading to the catastrophe. To give their particular names, they are, first, New

England, representing American history and tradition; second, Alaska and Africa, both frontiers in the sense of places ripe for economic development and exploitation; and third, New York, representing the city.

Let us take New England and examine its place in Willy's psychic as well as physical world. It is curious and significant that Willy, though late in life he is unable to make a living in New England, has nothing but good and kind thoughts about it. Earlier he had wanted to take the whole family there for a vacation. He never waxes rhapsodic about New York, but he does about New England. At times wistfulness and nostalgia come into his voice when he reminisces about New England. It has been the "field" that he has "ploughed"; it has yielded all the returns he has had for thirty years or more. It is "full of fine people" and "the cradle of the Revolution." To Willy, unlike New York, it is a place of historical significance in America; he even equates it with America. Instead of a geographical unit only, it is thus almost an essence to him, like the Pocahontas image, embodying an originally virginal and unspoiled America, in Hart Crane's *The Bridge.* Most important of all, it carries this high and imperishable image in Willy's mind; there old salesmen never die but only "fade away" to the hotel telephone where they carry on their extensive business amid increasing popularity and love. Willy's heartfelt description of the salesman over eighty who actually conducted business in this fashion suggests a worship of a state that appears as nothing less than the ideal. This is the salesman's Paradise. It may seem a tawdry one as Paradises go, but it may well be the best that a run-of-the-mill American salesman, with headquarters in New York in the mid-twentieth century, can imagine.

True, some of the deepest ironies of the play also develop from New England as the pole of "higher" value. For instance, as he gets older Willy can't make a living in it; New England is actually not one of the better sales territories. Willy presumably never makes enough in it to take his family on a vacation tour of its "beautiful towns." And as for its having "fine people" and being "the cradle of the Revolution," the positive side of both these values becomes in Willy's sales-soiled hands smirched and defaced; he commits adultery with one of these "fine people" and New England's vaunted "Revolution" thus becomes a merely personal, and sordid, infidelity.

Next, the frontier in the form of Alaska and Africa shapes up as a fairly constant "lower" pole of value, but still not the "lowest" (that is, the rockbottom level of negation of value). If New England looms as the "higher" pole, the yearned-for ideal, or almost "religion," in the extensive revision of the traditional epic and tragic scheme that *Death of a Salesman* presents, then with the same logic the frontier comes forth as representative of a "middle" pole. The middle stage in the long and tortuous development of value toward a point of refinement deserving of the name of "religion" is generally called "magic." And it is certainly the magical properties of the names of these two places, neither of which is any part of the play's actual setting, that are made use of. Alaska and Africa represent "heavens" all right, but only in the crudest, most materialistic form; they are really lands of quick riches only. It is because of their deep embuement with an almost exclusive appeal to the senses that they get so instantaneous a reaction from a Willy who has never quite had the heart to be a sourdough, ready to fight both for his own and the other fellow's. But, as the recurring images and conversations with the exploiter Ben show, the magical names of Alaska and Africa tantalize Willy constantly and actually sound the theme song of his "middle" world of values which eventually takes him to his "netherworld"—the region, that is, where all values, and even life itself, are frozen for good.

Our epic and tragic "universe," twentieth century American style, is now almost complete. What remains is only the "bottom" level, and that is the city, in this case New York. New York is the center of American business (America's chief day-to-day concern), and thus the natural "stand" of perhaps its most prevalent type, the salesman. New York is the infertile area, where seeds won't take root, though planted and replanted; where best friends go unrecognized; where infidelities are bred, though, in Willy's case, unconsummated (even an act of adultery, which is at least physically vital, is not possible for Willy in New York. "They don't need me in New York. I'm the New England man. I'm vital in New England."); where business loyalties and fair play do not last from one generation to another; where a gross premium is put on the showy, on success in a purely material or physical sense (witness Happy's financial and sexual success in this sense); and where, finally, sons like Happy, representing a basically infertile side of divided fathers like Willy, point up the play's traditionally tragic theme of a groping for self-knowledge by not even "knowing" their fathers when a luscious material or physical dividend catches and holds the eye. In brief, there is nothing about the city in this play that shows it to be anything but unfriendly to man, insidiously and increasingly so. Those who cope with it as Charley does do so by dint of a kind of philosophical legerdemain that leaves at least one side of their lives blank ("My salvation is that I never took any interest in anything."); the "whole" man does not grow in New York and New York is the last place to make a man "whole."

The scene in the restaurant, which may be considered the epitome of New York as here presented, comes closer to a picture of Hell than any other piece of modern literature—and certainly any other Realistic drama—I can think of. It is, in truth, the realm of "no-value," or of one value so pervasive that no other can survive beside it. Except for the still suffering and struggling Willy and Biff, everything in the restaurant is pure (though adept) negotiation with one and only one standard involved and and that is exclusively of the sense world. The "pick-ups," Happy, and worst of all the bartender Stanley (because he is purely servile even in this lurid realm of "rugged individualists" of the senses)—these recall classic scenes of descents into the abyss more sharply than anything else in twentieth century American literature. And Happy's casually curt lie about his collapsing father ("He's just a guy.") is surely as close to the tragic terror as anything in American drama has yet come.

In summary, the "world" or "universe" of *Death of a Salesman,* while representing vast rearrangements and shifts of poles of value, because of extraordinary changes in Western culture, especially as manifest in the United States, nevertheless still shows a basically traditional epic and tragic structure in that its poles of value are clearly located and distinguished one from another; in that they are also clearly objectified, as in the older tradition, but not allegorized, since Realistic drama stops short of tolerating allegory; and finally in that these poles of value, so located and objectified, precipitate the tragic situation and give a sense of a "universe" in the throes of unresolved conflict and agony.

Esther Merle Jackson

Death of a Salesman:
Tragic Myth in the Modern Theatre

Perhaps the dominant theme in the drama of the twentieth century is an attempt to recover—or, more precisely, to restate—a tragic apprehension about the human condition.[1] A pervasive concern about the ultimate meaning of human suffering is reflected, in one way or another, in the works of all of the major playwrights of the twentieth century: in those of Henrik Ibsen, August Strindberg, Anton Chekhov, George Bernard Shaw, Paul Claudel, John M. Synge, Fredrico Garcia Lorca, and Eugene O'Neill, as well as in those of Luigi Pirandello, Bertolt Brecht, Jean-Paul Sartre, Albert Camus, and more recently, Thornton Wilder, Tennessee Williams, Samuel Beckett, Jean Genet, Edward Albee, and others.

The American drama has been particularly concerned with the modern face

Reprinted from *CLA Journal, VII* (September, 1963), 63-76, by permission of the College Language Association and the author. Revised by the author for this publication.
[1] Miguel de Unamuno describes this perspective as the "tragic sense of life." See *Tragic Sense of Life,* trans. J. E. Crawford Flitch (New York, 1954).

of suffering. Since its emergence, barely a half-century ago, the American drama has attempted, rather consistently, to record the kinds of crises which have characterized our times. The great American masterworks—*Mourning Becomes Electra, The Time of Your Life, The Skin of Our Teeth, A Streetcar Named Desire*, and others—have been concerned with the response of mankind to rapid technological advance.[2] But the American dramatist has encountered serious difficulties in his search for a mode of expression appropriate to this theme. For he has been handicapped by a critical problem affecting communication: by the absence of a body of natural myths— symbolic interpretations of the life of man. Unlike Aeschylus, Shakespeare, Corneille, or subsequent playwrights in the interrelated European traditions, the American dramatist has been unable to employ as the instrumentation of his vision the great natural legends which are the residue of centuries of civilized growth.

The absence of conventional patterns of mythic interpretation has made it necessary for the American dramatist to devise new ways of seeing, interpreting, and recreating reality.[3] In terms of his ability to formulate coherent mythic patterns, perhaps the most effective dramatist in the American group is the "middle" playwright Arthur Miller. In his major works, *All My Sons, Death of a Salesman, The Crucible,* and *A View From the Bridge,* Miller seems to demonstrate a superiority to other American dramatists in the symbolic interpretation of universal dimensions of collective experience. Indeed, perhaps the most nearly mature myth about human suffering in an industrial age is Miller's masterwork, *Death of a Salesman.* In this work, first performed in 1949, Miller has formulated a statement about the nature of human crises in the twentieth century which seems, increasingly, to be applicable to the entire fabric of civilized experience. The superiority of *Death of a Salesman* over other worthy American dramas such as *Mourning Becomes Electra, A Streetcar Named Desire,* or Miller's own work, *The Crucible,* is the sensitivity of its myth: the critical relationship of its central symbol—the salesman—to the interpretation of the whole of contemporary life. In this image, Miller brings into the theatre a figure who is, in our age, a kind of hero—a ritual representative of an industrial society. It is its intimate association with our aspirations which gives to the story of Loman an ambiguous, but highly affecting, substratum of religious, philo-sophical, political, and social meanings. The appearance of the salesman

---

[2] See Doris V. Falk's discussion of *Eugene O'Neill and the Tragic Tension* (New Brunswick, New Jersey, 1958).

[3] Myth is particularly important to the drama, inasmuch as it provides a commonly accepted pattern of interpretation. It is a kind of *super-language,* through which many levels of content may be given simultaneous exposition. As the theatre is a "collective experience," this grounding of the narrative in a commonly understood symbology is of utmost importance to effective communication between author, actor, and spectator.

Loman as the subject of moral exploration stirs the modern spectator at that alternately joyful and painful periphery of consciousness which is the province of tragedy. The enactment of his suffering, fall, and partial enlightenment provokes a mixed response: that anger and delight, indignation and sympathy, pity and fear, which Aristotle described as "catharsis."

Miller writes that in Loman he has attempted to personify certain values which civilized men in the twentieth century share. The movement of tragedy from the ground of the lawless Titan Prometheus to that of the common man Loman does not represent, for Miller, a decline in values; on the contrary, it is evidence of a hopeful development. For Loman, a descendant of the nineteenth century protagonists of Ibsen, Chekhov, Shaw, and others, reflects Western civilization's increasing concern with a democratic interpretation of moral responsibilities. *Death of a Salesman* attempts to explore the implications of a life for which men—not gods—are wholly responsible.

Some of the problems with the interpretation of this play have grown out of the author's own statements about his intent; that is to say, Miller seems to have created in *Death of a Salesman* a form which transcended his conscious motives. *Death of a Salesman,* despite the presence of those social implications which Miller notes in his later essays, is a myth, not a document; that is to say, it is not, in the conventional sense, a problem play. Unlike Miller's earlier work *All My Sons, Death of a Salesman* is not concerned with such human failings as may find permanent social, political, or even psychological remedy. *Death of a Salesman,* like *The Crucible* and *A View From the Bridge,* is rather a study of a man's existence in a metaphysical universe. It is, like *Agamemnon, Oedipus the King, Hamlet,* and *King Lear,* a mythic apprehension of life. Willy Loman, like the traditional tragic protagonist, symbolizes the cruel paradox of human existence. His story, stripped to its mythic essentials, is familiar.

> An aged king—a pious man—moves toward life's end. Instead of reaping the benefits of his piety he finds himself caught in bewildering circumstances. Because of a mistake—an error in judgment—a tragic reversal has taken place in his life. Where he has been priest, knower of secrets, wielder of power, and symbol of life, he now finds himself adjudged defiler, usurper, destroyer, and necessary sacrifice. Like the traditional hero, Loman begins his long season of agony. In his descent, however, there is the familiar tragic paradox; for as he moves toward inevitable destruction, he acquires that knowledge, that sense of reconciliation, which allows him to conceive a redemptive plan for his house.[4]

As in traditional tragedy, Loman—the ritual head of his house—seeks to discover a design in the paradoxical movement of life; to impose upon it a

[4]See Arthur Miller, Introduction to *Arthur Miller's Collected Plays* (New York, 1957), pp. 30-36.

sense of meaning greater than that conferred upon it by actuality. The play asks the ancient questions: What real value is there in life? What evil resides in seeming good? What good is hidden in seeming evil? What permanence is buried beneath the face of change? What use can man make of his suffering?

Miller describes this drama as a study of the circumstances which affect human destiny in the moral universe:

> I take it that if one could know enough about a human being one could discover some conflict, some value, some challenge, however minor or major, which he cannot find it in himself to walk away from or turn his back on. The structure of these plays, in this respect, is to the end that such a conflict be discovered and clarified. Idea, in these plays, is the generalized meaning of that discovery applied to men other than the hero. Time, characterizations, and other elements are treated differently from play to play, but all to the end that that moment of commitment be brought forth, that moment when, in my eyes, a man differentiates himself from every other man, that moment when out of a sky full of stars he fixes on one star. I take it, as well, that the less capable a man is of walking away from the central conflict of the play, the closer he approaches a tragic existence. In turn, this implies that the closer a man approaches tragedy the more intense is his concentration of emotion upon the fixed point of his commitment . . . The assumption—or presumption—behind these plays is that life has meaning.[5]

Now the significant element in this statement is the playwright's suggestion that the ordinary actions of common men have ultimate meaning; that they are the concrete expression of conflict in the moral universe. The implication of this proposition is indeed profound. For it assigns primary responsibility for the conduct of the universe to man. Miller's position is, thus, opposed to that commonly assigned to Ibsen. Certainly, it is in contradiction to realism, which is concerned primarily with the meaning of action and being in a material world. It is, similarly, at variance with the philosophies posited by Christian dramatists such as Claudel and T. S. Eliot, who assign the larger role in the conduct of the universe to a divine power. Miller's position is, at this point, Sophoclean in nature. For like Sophocles, he suggests that the critical role in the moral universe is that of man himself.

Miller's classic stance is not singular in modern theatre. A study of the masterpieces of the last fifty years, both in Europe and in America, shows this classic concept of human responsibility to be common to many examples of contemporary drama. Miller's position is roughly parallel to that of Jean-Paul Sartre, who, in an earlier discussion of contemporary French theatre, wrote:

---

[5]*Ibid.,* pp. 7-8.

For them [the young playwrights] the theatre will be able to present man in his entirety only in proportion to the theatre's willingness to be *moral.* By that we do not mean that it should put forward examples illustrating the rules of deportment or the practical ethics taught to children, but rather that the study of the conflict of characters should be replaced by the presentation of the conflict of rights. . . . In each case it is, in the final analysis and in spite of divergent interests, the systems of values, of ethics, and of concepts of man which are lined up against each other. . . . This theatre does not give its support to any one 'thesis' and it's not inspired by any preconceived idea. All it seeks to do is to explore the state of man in its entirety and to present to the modern man a portrait of himself, his problems, his hopes, and struggles.[6]

Throughout the critical writings of the contemporaries—in the essays of O'Neill,[7] William Saroyan,[8] Wilder,[9] Williams,[10] and Arthur Miller,[11] as well as in the work of Europeans such as Sartre, Camus, and Jean Anouilh—. This dramatic motive is articulated: to illumine the moral choice which lies hidden beneath the face of actuality, to show modern man the present image of human destiny.

Now to say that Miller and others are in process of evolving a contemporary tragic myth is not to suggest that *Death of a Salesman* is an imitation of the Greek tragic form. Indeed, Miller states quite clearly that changes in the perception of universal law, as well as alterations in the very idea of man, would make Greek tragedy invalid as an expression of our time.[12] He writes that he seeks rather to evolve a form which may stand in the same kind of relationship to the moral crises of the twentieth century as did Greek, Shakespearean, and French tragic drama—each to its own epoch. While Miller and others appear, then, to have adopted certain characteristics belonging to traditional tragedy, they have rejected others. *Death of a Salesman* appears to imitate classic tragedy primarily in its acceptance of the principle of the ultimate responsibility of the individual.[13] That which appears to differentiate this work from traditional forms is its relocation of the tragic environment. For *Death of a Salesman,* like other examples of the contemporary genre, elevates to meaning a new protagonist: the common

---

[6] Jean-Paul Sartre, "Forgers of Myths," *Theatre Arts, XXX* (June, 1946), 329-30.
[7] See Eugene O'Neill, cited by Barrett H. Clark, in *Eugene O'Neill: the Man and His Plays* (New York, 1929), p. 130.
[8] See William Saroyan, Introduction to *The Time of Your Life* (London, 1942), pp. 5-12.
[9] See Thornton Wilder, Preface to *Three Plays* (New York, 1957), pp. vii-xiv.
[10] Tennessee Williams, Foreword to *Sweet Bird of Youth* (New York, 1959), pp. vii-xi.
[11] Arthur Miller, "On Social Plays," Preface to *A View From the Bridge* (London, 1960), pp. 7-24.
[12] Miller, Introduction to *Collected Plays,* p. 32.
[13] See also a transcript of an interview with Arthur Miller by Philip Gelb, "Morality and the Modern Drama," *Educational Theatre Journal,* X, no. 3 (October, 1958), 191-202.

man. Perhaps of greater importance is the fact that it removes the ground of the tragic conflict from outer event to inner consciousness.[14] Death of a *Salesman,* like *Mourning Becomes Electra, The Hairy Ape, A Streetcar Named Desire,* and others, may be described as a *tragedy of consciousness,* the imitation of a moral crisis in the life of a common man.

II

Miller traces this idea, in part, to the German expressionists, particularly, to Bertolt Brecht.[15] Professor John Gassner finds aspects of this "underground drama" in the nineteenth century innovators, not only in the works of Ibsen, Strindberg, Chekhov, and Shaw, but also in those of stream-of-consciousness novelists such as Dostoevsky, Tolstoy, and Henry James.[16] But while the contemporary dramatists are indebted to these sources, the idea of form as the *imitation of consciousness* is much older than the late nineteenth century. Clearly, Miller and others have borrowed heavily from Shakespeare and his antecedents in the liturgical drama; moreover, their interpretations of this internal struggle have some of their roots in both classic and neoclassic forms.[17]

The concept of tragedy as a crisis within the consciousness appears to have emerged clearly in the romantic period, particularly in the *Sturm und Drang* movement; in the theatres of Goethe, Schiller, Coleridge, Wagner, and Nietzsche. Oddly enough, the idea continued to dominate the theatre of the so-called "realists." It gained a systematic dramaturgy in expressionism; it has, throughout this century, intensified its hold upon the contemporary imagination. We may, thus, read the history of Western drama—classicism, neoclassicism, romanticism, realism, and expressionism—as a continuous development; the gradual narrowing of theatrical focus upon the moment of crisis within the individual consciousness.

The adoption of this concept of drama as the imitation of consciousness accounted for major alterations in form. The contemporary form is not a representation of ordinary modes of action, an imitation of events-in-themselves. It is rather concerned with the representation of consciousness,

---

[14]The principle of interpretation involved in the idea of a tragic action which progresses within the consciousness was given early exposition by the philosopher Søren Kierkegaard, in his essay "Ancient Tragical Motif." See *Either/Or,* trans. David F. and Lillian M. Swenson (Garden City, New York, 1959), pp. 138-62.

[15]Miller, Introduction to *Collected Plays,* pp. 39-45.

[16]John Gassner, *The Theatre in Our Times* (New York, 1954), pp. 349-50.

[17]Aristotle discusses a level of dramatic conflict which he describes as "internal." However, the Greek dramatists did not appear to regard this internal level as the major focus of dramatic interest. There is some evidence that it tended to grow more important in the later plays of Sophocles and Euripides. Witness the change in form in works such as *Oedipus at Colonus* and *Orestes.*

with the imitation of a single moment of experience. We may describe *Death of a Salesman,* for example, as a theatrical illusion. For it is intended, according to Miller, as the apparition of a key image, the imitation of the "way of mind" which characterizes the Salesman Willy:

> The first image that occurred to me which was to result in *Death of a Salesman* was of an enormous face the height of the proscenium arch which would appear and then open up, and we would see the inside of a man's head. . . . The *Salesman* image was from the beginning absorbed with the concept that nothing in life comes "next" but that everything exists together and at the same time within us; that there is no past to be "brought forward" in a human being, but that he is his past at every moment and that the present is merely that which his past is capable of noticing and smelling and reacting to.
>
>   I wished to create a form which, in itself as a form, would literally be the process of Willy Loman's way of mind.[18]

Death of a Salesman, as vision, follows an aesthetic rather than a logical mode of development. For it represents the protagonist's attempt to reconstitute the progression of his experience. Loman, as the protagonist, has an extremely complicated identity; for he is actor-observer-creator. As actor, he is the very ground of reality—the shape of experience itself; at the same time, he is the observer of that unique vision. He is required, finally, to be a creator, the architect of a new poetic universe in which all components of his vision are united in a harmonious entity.

We may describe this kind of structure as a theatrical realization of the stream of consciousness. Miller's stream of consciousness differs in certain particulars from that of other dramatists such as Williams and O'Neill; it is, in many ways, close to the visions of novelists such as Virginia Woolf. For, like Woolf, Miller does not divide his vision of reality into discrete units—pictures with rigid boundaries. He, rather, conceives Willy's mind as a place "out of time," as a state in which all boundaries have been erased, in which all things are coexistent. He writes: "Above all, in the structural sense, I aimed to make a play with the veritable countenance of life. To make the one the many . . ."[19]

Now, the need to give such an ambiguous poetic perception a concrete form in the theatre has, obviously, presented the playwright with a difficult problem which other American dramatists have shared: How can "consciousness" be connoted on the stage?[20] As in traditional tragedy, Miller projects

---

[18]Miller, Introduction to *Collected Plays,* pp. 23-24.
[19]*Ibid.,* p. 30.
[20]The Americans have evolved a conventional scheme of representation which may be described as a "psychological syntax." While Europeans such as Giraudoux, Sartre, Camus, and others have followed a philosophical orientation in giving to consciousness

his vision of experience by employing the methods of poetry. *Death of a Salesman,* like *Prometheus Bound, Oedipus, King Lear,* or, for that matter, *Ghosts, The Cherry Orchard, The Ghost Sonata, The Hairy Ape, Our Town,* or *A Streetcar Named Desire,* is thus a kind of poem; that is to say, it represents the exposition of a key image through the simultaneous realization of component figures. We have noted Miller's own comment on the central image of Willy's head, which opens up to reveal his "way of mind." He describes the play as a veritable "sea of images"—shapes in the protagonist's vision:

> The play's eye was to revolve from within Willy's head, sweeping endlessly in all directions like a light on the sea, and nothing that formed in the distant mist was to be left uninvestigated. It was thought of as having the density of the novel form in its interchange of viewpoints, so that while all roads led to Willy the other characters were to feel it was their play, a story about them and not him.[21] . . . There are no flashbacks in this play but only a mobile concurrency of past and present, and this, again, because in his desperation to justify his life Willy Loman has de-destroyed the boundaries between now and then. . . .[22]

Death of a Salesman is an aesthetic progression: a reconstruction of the movement of consciousness: the perception of facts, events, and ideas; fears, passions, and superstitions; hopes, dreams, and ambitions, in their various stages of maturity and immaturity.[23] Clearly, this definition might easily apply to other contemporary arts, particularly, to the novel, the long poem, the modern dance, or the cinema. The significant factor which distinguishes *Death of a Salesman* from these related forms is the fact that it was written to be spoken and performed by live actors before a live audience. Miller speaks of drama as a symbolic ritual which projects the spectator's consciousness into the mind of the protagonist, and which, in turn, introjects the suffering,

---

the shape of organized thought—the logic of discursive language—the Americans have tended to interpret perception in terms of extrarational faculties as a function of the subconscious mind. American dramatists, historically concerned with faculties such as the *will* and the *imagination,* have been inclined throughout the entire period of the theatre's development to stress the role of these drives and responses generally described as "irrational." It is for this and other reasons that certain of the patterns of thought and language associated with the work of Sigmund Freud, Carl G. Jung, and others have been of use to American playwrights as elements of a conventional mode of interpretation for a mythic apprehension of reality. Much of the linguistic structure through which Miller connotes Loman's suffering, his enlightenment, and his tragic triumph is, in this sense, psychological in its origin. But it is important to observe, however, that this language is descriptive in its function; that is to say, it shows us *how* Loman suffers, but not *why.*
21Miller, Introduction to *Collected Plays,* p. 30.
22*Ibid.,* p. 26.
23Stephen's discussion of this aesthetic principle, in James Joyce, *The Portrait of an Artist as a Young Man* (London, 1916), p. 241.

enlightenment, and triumph of the protagonist into the consciousness of the spectator. Miller, like other contemporary dramatists, regards *spectacle* as a critical element of theatrical language. For it provides the poetic vision with its sensuous fabric, with its texture.

Miller, like other playwrights who have followed the theories and practice of Richard Wagner, has given considerable attention to the articulation of an appropriate dramaturgy for the interpretation of his tragic myth.[24] Much of the text of *Death of a Salesman* is given to the articulation of the sensuous form of the poetic image. The playwright's description of the setting follows:

> *A melody is heard, played upon a flute. It is small and fine, telling of grass and trees and the horizon. The curtain rises.*
> *Before us is the Salesman's house. We are aware of towering, angular shapes behind it, surrounding it on all sides. Only the blue light of the sky falls upon the house and forestage; the surrounding area shows an angry glow of orange. As more light appears, we see a solid vault of apartment houses around the small, fragile-seeming home. An air of the dream clings to the place, a dream rising out of reality. . . .*
> *The entire setting is wholly or, in some places, partially transparent. The roof-line of the house is one-dimensional; under and over it we see the apartment buildings. Before the house lies an apron, curving beyond the forestage into the orchestra. This forward area serves as the back yard as well as the locale of all Willy's imaginings and of his city scenes. Whenever the action is in the present the actors observe the imaginary wall-lines, entering the house only through its door at the left. But in the scenes of the past these boundaries are broken, and characters enter or leave a room by stepping "through" a wall onto the forestage.*[25]

Death of a Salesman is, then, an example of that kind of form which Professor Francis Fergusson has described as "poetry in the theatre."[26] It is a myth which projects before the spectator an image of the protagonist's consciousness. The playwright attempts to reveal a tragic progression within that consciousness. He employs, as the instrumentation of vision, a complex theatre symbol: a union of gesture, word, and music; light, color, and pattern; rhythm and movement.[27] We may now ask: What is the nature of Miller's myth? In what sense is it tragic?

---

[24]It is useful to compare Miller's discussions of theatrical form with those of Richard Wagner, in *Opera and Drama* trans. Edwin Evans, 2 vols. (London, 1913).

[25]Miller, Stage Directions, *Death of a Salesman* in *Arthur Miller's Collected Plays* (New York, 1957), pp. 130-31.

[26]Professor Fergusson paraphrases the language of Jean Cocteau in his discussion "Poetry of the Theater and the Poet in the Theater" in *The Idea of a Theater* (Princeton, New Jersey, 1962), pp. 194-228.

[27]See Antonin Artaud, *The Theatre and Its Double,* trans. Mary Caroline Richards (New York, 1958), pp. 37-47.

III

Miller follows O'Neill in suggesting that suffering in the modern world is often deceptively masked, inasmuch as it has been clearly removed from the context of the purely physical. The contemporary protagonist Loman suffers from such an ambiguous evil, from a malady which modern arts and letters have determined the moral sickness of the twentieth century. Miller describes this sickness as the "disease of unrelatedness." Its symptoms are a sense of alienation, a loss of meaning, and a growing despair. We have seen this illness personified in protagonists throughout the contemporary drama: in O'Neill's Yank, Williams's Blanche, Wilder's Henry Artrobus in *The Skin of Our Teeth,* as well as in the protagonists of Clifford Odets, Saroyan, Lillian Hellman, Lorraine Hansberry, and, more recently, Edward Albee. While other dramatists are often equivocal in their assessment of causes, Miller is quite clear about the roots of this sickness. He traces modern suffering to the ancient cause: ignorance. *Death of a Salesman* attempts to trace Loman's progress from ignorance through the cycle of suffering to enlightenment. As in classic tragedy, the price of this odyssey is death, but, through his personal sacrifice, the protagonist redeems his house and promises to his posterity yet another chance.

Miller's transposition of the tragic movement to a "modern key" seems effective. If there is a problem with his myth, it would seem to emanate from his choice of Loman as protagonist; that is to say, with the idea of a truly common man as tragic hero. For at first glance, Willy Loman, as a symbol of modern man, seems to have critical shortcomings. To begin with, he does not seem to have sinned greatly enough to satisfy the needs of tragic shock and terror. In this respect, Tennessee Williams's protagonists, with their sexual crimes, more nearly approach the Greek interpretation of man sickened by the horror of transgression. Miller's *hamartia* is more subtle than that of Williams and perhaps more Classic in its ultimate implications. For Miller, like Sophocles, insists that tragic catastrophe is the result of ignorance rather than the end of willful transgression. Loman's crime in the universe may be likened to that of Agamemnon or Lear; it is the appearance of indifference, the absence of sympathy, and the lack of a sense of moral law. For Miller, moral ignorance is at once, the most serious—and most common—indictment against humanity in our time.

But there is, yet, a second and even more serious objection which may be raised againt Loman as hero; and that is that he does not seem to measure up to the stature of a great and good man. Against the outline of Oedipus, Lear, or Faust, Loman appears a small man, a mere failure who does not have sufficient grace to warrant universal concern. Again, appearances belie the truth. For Loman, Miller holds, is the measure of critical changes in value associated with the rise of a democratic society. It is, according to the playwright, Loman who is the symbol of the most powerful moral force in the modern world: the common man. It is, the playwright continues, the outcome of the crisis within his consciousness which will, with certainty, determine the disposition of the moral dilemma which still grips the human race. But Miller the American goes even further in the justification of his protagonist. For, he declares, not only must a contemporary tragic myth mirror the shape of transgression and the nature of power in our age, it ought also to be the measure of our ethical advance over prior civilizations. If the Greek hero mirrored a society which condoned slavery, and the Renaissance protagonist represented an aristocratic minority, Willy Loman is the measure of democracy's promise of unlimited human possibility. He is the representative of an open order where all values—even virtue—may be gained at any moment when a man is willing to risk commitment.

It is clear that, for Miller, Loman is a virtuous man; that is to say, he wins virtue, in a moment released from the boundaries of time and causality. Miller, like the existentialists, defines virtue, heroism, and nobility, in anti-Aristotelian terms; that is to say, Loman's character is not a static arrangement of fixed virtues. On the contrary, the protagonist gains ultimate value in the universe at the same instant when he commits himself to the search for truth, in that "existential moment" which the play itself represents. Loman, the contemporary hero, embarks upon a most courageous odyssey, the descent into the self, where he engages his most dangerous enemy, himself. The fact that he does so late in his life does not, in the contemporary context, diminish his value. For Loman, like Lear, is a hero who comes late in the tragic progression to enlightenment.

Miller attempts to take his tragic cycle to its natural conclusion by giving a sign to the protagonist's victory. In *Death of a Salesman,* as in traditional tragedy, the sign is itself a paradox. Loman's suicide, like Oedipus's self-blinding or Antigone's self-murder, is obviously intended as a gesture of the hero's victory over circumstances. It is an act of love, intended to redeem his house. Willy's wife indicates this interpretation in the Requiem:

Forgive me, dear, I can't cry. I don't know what it is, but I can't cry. I don't understand it. Why did you ever do that? Help me, Willy. I can't cry. It seems to me that you're just on another trip. I keep expecting you. Willy, dear, I can't cry. Why did you do it? I search and search and I search, and I can't understand it, Willy. I made the last payment on the house today. Today, dear. And there'll be nobody home. . . . We're free and clear. . . . We're free. . . . We're free. . . . We're free. . . .[28]

---

[28] Miller, *Death of a Salesman,* in *The Collected Plays,* p. 222.

Arthur Miller's *Death of a Salesman* is, perhaps, the most mature example of a dramatic myth about contemporary life to emerge in American theatre to this time. The chief value of this drama is its attempt to reveal those ultimate meanings which are resident in modern experience. Perhaps the most significant comment on this play is not its literary achievement, as such, but is rather the impact which it has had on spectators, both in America and abroad. The influence of this drama, first performed in 1949, continues to grow in world theatre. For it articulates, in a language which can be appreciated by popular audiences, certain new dimensions of the human dilemma. The playwright's own words would seem to summarize the achievement of this myth about modern life:

> The ultimate justification for a genuine new form is the new and heightened consciousness it creates and makes possible—a consciousness of causation in the light of known but hitherto inexplicable effects.[29]

This essay, originally written in 1960, was published in 1963. I have made slight adjustments here and there, but no substantial revisions.

Esther M. Jackson
Madison, 1971

---

[29] Miller, Introduction to *Collected Plays,* p. 53.

Gordon W. Couchman

Arthur Miller's Tragedy of Babbitt

If we accept Walpole's distinction concerning life as it appears to those who think and those who feel, we must accept the classification of satire as comedy. Pursuing the matter further, however, we are bound to see that although satire begins as comedy it does not always end as comedy; if the mission of satire is to hold the mirror up to folly and vice, then we might conclude that true comedy never can be satirical at all, since from folly and vice (or so the moralists assure us) come pain and evil, and pain and evil suggest not comedy but tragedy. Unlike comedy in the ordinary sense, satire exposes a weakness which may be fatal. Tragedy on the other hand,

---

Reprinted from *Educational Theatre Journal, VII* (October, 1955), 206-11, by permission of the American Educational Theatre Association and the author.

understood as the depiction of individual suffering, while far from excluding the satirical (witness *Hamlet*), does not ordinarily seek so much to expose the weakness as to redeem it through some compensatory quality of greatness. But if, as in bourgeois tragedy, not only the weakness of the individual, but also of the society, that produced him, is at least implied, to that extent tragedy itself may assume more of the character of satire, which is always, inferentially, a social matter.

It is significant that, even though Theodore Dreiser in 1925 called his most famous novel *An American Tragedy,* much of American literature in the 1920's was satirical. Equally significant is the fact that for our own time the brittle, brilliant satire of a Mencken or a Lewis no longer appears either appropriate or adequate. It is not too much to say that the bright little world portrayed in the opening paragraph of *Babbitt* is almost as remote from the stream-lined America of today as the world of that other satirist, Mark Twain. Even more than Lewis's generation has ours had to suffer from the brassy noise of high-pressure commercialism and a Janus-faced technological advance beside which Babbitt's worship of gadgets seems innocence itself. It comes as something of a shock to realize that in rereading *Babbitt,* published in 1922, we are, to all intents, back in the days before radio (to say nothing of radio and television networks), before supermarkets on any such scale as today, before air travel as we know it today. A hundred phenomena might be cited to suggest the change which has come over America since the era of Babbitt, but none would tell us any more than the plain statement that the things that Babbitt represents are no longer as simple as they appeared to the Lewises and the Menckens, nor as funny. What was once a subject for satire in the comic sense, the overemphasis on externals, seems now a matter for more sober reflection.

It would not be surprising, therefore, if to present-day readers, Sinclair Lewis's satire on George F. Babbitt in the nineteen-twenties should seem less amusing than instructive. Today we are likely to hear chiefly the "sadder and deeper notes" that Ludwig Lewisohn in *Expression in America* hears in this "brilliant and contemptuous satiric presentation." Thus the noisy reunion of Babbitt's class of '96 has a parallel, insofar as a parallel exists at all, in the blank and silent luncheon meeting of fellow-alumni which Marquand's *H. M. Pulham, Esq.,* attends two decades later. In reality, readers who seek a successor to Babbitt in contemporary satire are likely to come away disappointed. Babbitt's real successor has other origins. His name is Willy Loman.

A recent query by Joseph Wood Krutch in *The Saturday Review* for January 10, 1953, "Is Our Common Man Too Common?" suggests the possibility that the malady which *Babbitt* was written to expose if not to cure (though the example here is my own), may merely have taken a new and more distrubing turn. If this is so, it is appropriate that George F. Babbitt today should be not the target of satire but the protagonist in a tragedy. Moreover, as the novel has a notable lineage in middle-class satire, so the play has a long and illustrious ancestry in English bourgeois tragedy, in which the fate of the hero, as suggested above, is to some extent a commentary on the social conditions which helped to make it possible. As for the respective forms of drama and fiction, pertinent aspects of Babbittry itself were being satirized on the stage during the Babbitt era in Eugene O'Neill's William Brown and Marco, Elmer Rice's Mr. Zero, and even in George Kelly's showoff, Aubrey Piper. Willy Loman has predecessors in the drama who already are blood-brothers to George F. Babbitt, and the circumstance that Willy is the hero of a play and Babbitt the hero of a novel is really incidental. Of far greater importance is the fact that, in an age in which Babbitt's ideals are an anachronism, Willy is incapable of any other. Thus Arthur Miller merely brings Sinclair Lewis up to date.

As Ludwig Lewisohn has noted, Sinclair Lewis's novel has a definite structure, an example of which is the purposeful balance within Chapters XV and XIX. In spite of, or perhaps because of this neat structure, *Babbitt* could almost be taken apart and rearranged as two books. One of these books would be about George F. Babbitt, but the other would be about Babbittry, for which the hackneyed phrase, the worship of Success, is still the closest equivalent. Lewis's satire is simply the story of what Babbittry does to George F. Babbitt. Arthur Miller's tragedy is the story of what it does to Willy Loman.

"Babbitt" and "Babbittry" during the nineteen-twenties became, if not household words, at least epithets to conjure with in many a divided household. Likewise "Many Americans," according to John Gassner in his introduction to *Death of a Salesman* in *A Treasury of The Theatre,* "from all walks of life have identified themselves or their relatives with Willy . . . ." Babbittry destroys the best that is in George F. Babbitt, and consumes Willy Loman. Babbitt is a salesman first and last. Babbitt glories in his commonplaceness; nothing terrifies him more than not to be thought one of the boys. Willy, with his "jolly locker-room personality," as Gassner phrases it, might have been one of Babbitt's salesmen.

The city that makes Babbitt (and even his creator) exult, closes in on Willy, robs him of his self-respect, gives him an excuse for complaining but no excuse for living. "We don't belong in this nuthouse of a city," protests his son Biff. The ideal of salesmanship that sustains Babbitt through flights of Booster oratory and orgies of backslapping, produces Howard Wagner, who thinks more of his new wire-recorder than he does of his oldest salesman. Babbitt's worship of success becomes an obsession in Willy, and when success almost visibly slips through his fingers, he transfers his ideal to his son, on whom it sits as a burden intolerable as death. Babbitt's easy business ethics are a cynical corruption in Willy. Willy ordering his own sons to steal sand from a nearby construction job is only one example. This he does for the benefit of their rich uncle Ben. Ben's voice in fact booms through the jungle of Willy's confusions, as through the jungle of Africa, a hollow reminder of that success which has not so much eluded Willy as tricked him into thinking he is what he is not. Babbitt also—he who fawns upon the McKelveys and subsides into awed silence before banker Eathorne—would have been hypnotized by Ben.

Ben is a living reminder to Willy of what might have been. "If I'd gone with him to Alaska that time," Willy tries to convince himself, "everything would've been totally different." Babbitt tells us that he too has not done what he wanted to do. "I could have been a darn good orator," he complains to Myra. Seneca Doane, the "radical" lawyer, appeases Babbitt's antagonisms but not his discontents when he says to him: "I remember—in college you were an unusually liberal, sensitive chap. I can still recall your saying to me that you were going to be a lawyer, and take the cases of the poor for nothing, and fight the rich." To his son Ted at the end Babbitt makes the most damaging admission of all: "Practically, I've never done a single thing I've wanted to in my whole life."

To George F. Babbitt the man comes doubts from time to time concerning Babbittry itself. In his fumbling for some answer to his questions Babbitt becomes most nearly a person, individualized, humanized, understandable in suffering. At such moments the satire is almost stilled, and one can hear distinctly an undertone of melancholy that pervades Willy Loman's story. But though in his more inward moments Babbitt may see himself as a failure, outwardly he is a Success, both in his own estimation and that of Zenith. No matter how strenuously Willy strives to persuade himself otherwise, being fired by the son of the man who had hired him merely confirms an inner conviction of total failure. Willy is Babbitt with the corners of the mask turned down. Babbitt merely wants to be liked: Willy wants to be *well*-liked. With this criterion he has inspired his sons. The tragedy becomes explicit when Charley, Willy's only friend, demands: "Willy, why must everybody like you?"—a question for which Willy has no answer. Fortunately for Babbitt, Paul Riesling is not a Charley.

Perhaps nothing so well illustrates the evolution from Babbitt to Willy Loman as the friendships of the two men. For all Babbitt's dread of not being one of the boys, his one real friend, Paul Riesling, is a "highbrow." Babbitt loves Paul with single-minded devotion.

He was fonder of Paul Riesling than of anyone on earth except himself and his daughter Tinka. They had been classmates, roommates, in the

State University, but always he thought of Paul Riesling, with his dark slimness, his precisely parted hair, his nose-glasses, his hesitant speech, his moodiness, his love of music, as a younger brother, to be petted and protected.

When Paul goes to prison for shooting his nagging wife, Zilla, Babbitt loses the one member of his adult world whose welfare means more to him than his own, his sole refuge from "the pomposities of being Mr. George F. Babbitt of Zenith." He visits Paul in prison: "Babbitt knew that in this place of death Paul was already dead. And as he pondered on the train home something in his own self seemed to have died."

Thus Babbitt, in a relationship of comparative simplicity, *gives*. Willy, in a friendship with Charley as complex as the other is simple, *takes*. If any brothering is done, Charley does it, but one cannot imagine Willy admitting such a thing. Willy treats Charley as one of the family; that is, he quarrels with Charley constantly. Yet he himself tells Charley: "You're the only friend I got." It is Charley who in the hour of Willy's defeat sums up the fatal befuddlement that is Willy: "And the funny thing is that you're a salesman, and you don't know that." All the sentimental protective charm of single-minded devotion in which Babbitt luxuriates is gone, its place taken by the recriminations of men moving about in worlds dimly realized. Informed by Charley that his son Bernard is to argue a case before the Supreme Court, Willy can only marvel that Bernard has not even mentioned it. The reason is quite simple to Charley: "He don't have to—he's gonna do it." Friendship with a Paul Riesling pales alongside the massive reality of having Charley for your neighbor.

As we have seen, Babbitt faces himself with surprising resolution if not very satisfactory results. In spite of his boasting, Willy, too, is more than once brought up short against an image of himself which is far from flattering. "You know, the trouble is, Linda, people don't seem to take to me." People laugh at him or ignore him altogether.

> I'm fat. I'm very—foolish to look at, Linda. I didn't tell you, but Christmas time I happened to be calling on F. H. Stewarts and a salesman I know, as I was going in to see the buyer I heard him say something about—walrus. And I—I cracked him right across the face. I won't take that. I simply will not take that. But they do laugh at me. I know that.

After he has been fired, Willy interrupts his conversation with Bernard to ask in a small voice, "What's the secret?" When Ben tells Willy that the latter's suicide will be called cowardly, Willy rejoins: "Why? Does it take more guts to stand here the rest of my life ringing up a zero?" Willy jeers at Hap's fatuous attempts to reassure him. And yet Willy never really faces either the paternal corruption apparent in Hap, whom his mother herself calls a philandering bum, or the corruption which conditions Biff to steal Bill Oliver's fountain pen.

Of George F. Babbitt one might say unhesitatingly that he makes out all right. Willy Loman's story, as we said at the beginning of this study, suggests that the problem of Babbittry is no longer so simple. Babbitt and his son Ted—"the Babbitt men"—join forces at the end. Of his own volition, and while still in most respects a boy, Ted leaves college to marry, and although he is ignorant of his father's clumsy philanderings, nothing in his upbringing or environment would indicate that he would necessarily disapprove. On the other hand Biff, thirty-four, never finishes high school because in a squalid Boston hotel room he saw his father, not as dad who could be counted on to "fix" a failure in math., but as Willy Loman who gave a woman stockings which rightfully belonged to Biff's mother. The shallow, sheepish understandings of "the Babbitt men" give way to mortal combat between Biff and Willy. In the last scene with Ben Willy asks:

> Oh, Ben, how do we get back to all the great times? Used to be so full of light, and comradeship, the sleigh-riding in winter, and the ruddiness on his cheeks. And always some kind of good news coming up, always something nice coming up ahead. And never even let me carry the valises in the house, and simonizing, simonizing that little red car! Why can't I give him something and not have him hate me?

Here Willy echoes Linda's anguished query to Biff earlier in the play: "Why are you so hateful to each other? Why is that?" The answer lies in the corruption which is Willy's heritage to Biff. "I stole myself out of every good job since high school," exclaims Biff in the showdown. But the corruption goes deeper even than this. "We never told the truth for ten minutes in this house!" When Willy arrives at the restaurant to have dinner with Happy and Biff, the latter has had six hours of cooling his heels in Bill Oliver's office to learn some home truths about himself. "Who was it, pop?" he demands. "Who ever said I was a salesman with Oliver?" From this it is only a step to the showdown, when Biff shouts at his father: "I never got anywhere because you blew me so full of hot air I could never stand taking orders from anybody!" During this showdown one can hear a woman's laughter from an earlier scene, half-strident, half-voluptuous, blaring through a mounting storm of accusations: Biff's stealing, cheating, roughing the girls, driving without a license. . . .

From this agony of father and son groping toward each other through the nightmare of their mutual disenchantment, Linda could not escape if she wished: she is wife and mother, judge and comforter, hopelessly involved. By comparison, Myra Babbitt plays a passive role, at times holding her own only with difficulty against the incorrigible patronizing of twin male egos. Myra is possessive enough in a dumb, dogged way, and capable of quietly doing as she pleases in the matter of the McKelvey dinner invitations, but she usually succeeds in registering mere token protests against her husband's domineering ways. Linda is Willy's apologist: "Attention—attention must be paid to such a man." But she is more: to his sons she is conscience itself, she fixes responsibility for actions, something which, according to the playwright himself, must be done if our theater is to recover the spirit of tragedy: "You're a pair of animals! Not one, not another living soul would have had the cruelty to walk out on that man in a restaurant!" This is undeniably a new voice in our theater. As Eugene O'Neill once put it, the playwright whose characters speak like this is seeking to do more than merely scribble around the surface of things. Steadfastly refusing to deceive herself in the midst of all the self-deception around her, Linda seems always to be waiting fatalistically for the next blow. It is Linda who worries about Biff's stealing, who asks why Biff must fight, who distrusts Ben. Between Myra Babbitt's whimpering about not being wanted and Linda's quiet lament over Willy's grave a revolution has taken place, a revolution which no mere difference in talent or medium can account for. Myra Babbitt has on her hands a successful child; Linda seeks to protect a failure who must nevertheless be reckoned a man. A length of rubber hose measures the distance between the two situations.

But in order fully to understand the wedded life of Mr. and Mrs. George F. Babbitt, we have to know the fairy girl. The fairy girl, slim and white, waits for Babbitt in his dreams. In his waking hours she is by turns his secretary, his provocative teen-age future daughter-in-law, the wife of one of the boys, finally a customer, Tanis Junique. In the midst of his most painful introspections Babbitt "stumbled onto the admission that he wanted the fairy girl—in the flesh." He becomes conscious of a longing "to run childishly with his troubles to the comfort of the fairy child." And when he meets Tanis Junique he exults: "I've found her! I've dreamed of her all these years and now I've found her!" No matter that this vision, like his marriage itself, cannot survive the reality.

To Louetta Swanson, one of the women whom he identifies with the fairy girl, Babbitt confesses that he is "always lonely." To Biff in the hotel room Willy explains feebly: "She's nothing to me, Biff. I was lonely, I was terribly lonely." But instead of a fairy girl's slivery chime Willy hears through Linda's well-meaning laughter the laughter of Linda's Boston rival, who will "put him right through to the buyers." Instead of pursuing a fairy child, Willy is obliged in front of Biff's shattered eyes to give Linda's stockings to The Woman in order to get rid of her. Throughout Babbitt's quest for the fairy girl, disaster, it is true, never seems far off, but it never quite catches up, and Babbitt is restored snug and secure to the bosom of his family and the Good

Citizens' League. Disaster breaks rudely over Willy's head. "I'll make it up to you," he says half-heartedly to Linda, but the sight of her mending has the effect of an apparition: "I won't have you mending stockings in this house!" To Biff and later to Ben he confesses almost pleadingly: "The woman has waited and the woman has suffered. . . ." For Willy there is no fairy girl, only Biff to call him a fake and a dime a dozen.

Willy Loman, says John Gassner in the introduction quoted earlier, is a victim of "overpublicized" values.

> Insofar as it exposes the hollowness of materialistic values, *Death of a Salesman* carries on the cultural rebellion staged by the playwrights, novelists, critics, and artists of the nineteen-twenties.

As others have pointed out, Sinclair Lewis's hatred of Babbittry did not prevent him from being more than half in love with George F. Babbitt and the city of Zenith itself. Whether or not, as Alfred Kazin asserts in *On Native Grounds*, Lewis later succumbed to the attitudes he had ridiculed, is immaterial, as is the charge heard elsewhere that Willy Loman's story is not tragic because the playwright himself despises Willy's values. Arthur Miller himself has discussed this subject at some length, but his own Linda sums it up: "A little man can be just as exhausted as a great man." Babbitt and his descendant alike, when one comes right down to it, had the "wrong dreams," but, each in his blundering way works out a solution of a kind. Babbitt's hope is in his son Ted, and Willy's in Biff; the interval that separates the two endings in time makes it inevitable that, whatever the difference in emotional response may be, we are willing to accept Babbitt's solution, while Willy's seems as troubled and confused as the age itself.

And yet, one almost feels that the note of reconciliation on which the novel ends must have been of less consequence before the same mood found such memorable expression in the play. At its best, Arthur Miller's play shares with Sinclair Lewis's novel a rare gift for the poetic in the colloquial which redeems both works from being merely depressing. What Willy's friend, Charley, would have said of Babbitt's dreams we can only surmise, but for Willy we know that he pronounces, in his own unique idiom, the only fitting epitaph.

4. Characters

Guerin Bliquez

Linda's Role in *Death of a Salesman*

Mrs. Willy Loman has a more forceful role in *Death of A Salesman* than most commentators have thus far noted. To overlook the part she plays in her husband's pathetic downfall is to miss one of the most profound levels in Arthur Miller's subtle structuring of his tragedy. Linda's facility for prodding Willy to his doom is what gives the play its direction and its impetus.

Death of a Salesman is more than the story of one man's failure. Its theme includes the disintegration of a family in a particular social world, brought about by self-blindness and a refusal to know or to acknowledge others. It demonstrates how a fear of the responsibilities of knowledge can lead only to ruin. Miller's ironic rendering of Linda as the bulwark deserves closer examination.

The Lomans have been married almost thirty-five years. They have reared two sons. Although during most of that time Willy was on the road for as much as five days every week, his absences cannot provide sufficient reason for the terrible mutual ignorance that he and Linda share. This couple is not alienated, in the usual sense of that term. They never fight or disagree. All outward appearances demonstrate an intimate relationship and a secure marriage. Even their sons are unable to see that a great part of Linda's married life has been devoted to the task of helping Willy shirk the responsibilities of the kind of knowledge needed to hold himself and his family together.

Willy is a dreamer. What joys he has are always projections into a friendly heaven that is ignorant of a hostile earth. This salesman never learns to know his territory, his ideals of the workaday world notwithstanding. His labors are heroic, almost, and always aimed at financial-social success. But faithful Linda helps to insure only their marginal return.

Objectively Linda is the proof of her husband's ability as provider and subjectively the negation of it. She is his security symbol. Centered as she is in the house and garden, she is in a way identical with these as the empirical fact of Willy's success as a breadwinner. But subjectively, Linda makes demands. Thematically, she is the source of the cash-payment fixation. Like the house and garden, she must be constantly secured, maintained, planted, and cultivated. She is the goal of the salesman's futile activity as a man, a goal that can never be achieved.

Willy of course is unaware of this. He thinks his sons are the principal reason for his drive. But all he can give them is his platitudes and a punching bag. He has no real time for them; he is still trying to woo their mother.

Reprinted from *Modern Drama*, X (February, 1968), 383-86, by permission of the journal and of A. C. Edwards.

In his stage directions Miller explains that "Linda . . . has developed an iron repression to Willy's behavior—she more than loves him, she admires him." These two characteristics—repression and love—transcending admiration—are the forces by which Willy is seriously undermined at home.

To appreciate Linda's repression demands an understanding of the difference between acceptance and acquiescence. Significantly, it is a difference in degrees of knowledge. Acceptance of reality is an active state of cognition. Acquiescence is passive. Understanding plays no part. A wife cannot acquiesce morally to a husband's serious faults. If Linda accepts Willy for what he is shown to be, she accepts a liar, a cheat, and a pompous fraud. Such attributes cannot be explained away, as Linda tries to do, by her husband's exhaustion. Add the note of potential suicide, which Linda is "ashamed" to expose because it would be an "insult," and we are all the more suspicious of her real conception of Willy. To acquiesce in all of Willy's weaknesses is to be a failure as a wife and mother, and to share in the responsibility of her husband's fall.

The second characteristic of Linda's relationship to her husband is even more destructive. How is it possible in marriage for admiration to reach a point of "more than" love? If all admiration is grounded in love—if not love of a particular person, at least love of the values exemplified—how can admiration be transcendent? But if in this marriage admiration does transcend love, then it follows that for Linda the superiority of her husband is more important than any marital equality. This is hero projection on her part. It is to insure this superiority that Linda does not support her husband where he is weak. To do this would confirm her status as an equal partner with her own specific role and would provide a dialectical "other" that would synthesize Willy as a complete man. Instead, Linda "has developed an iron repression" that constantly belittles Willy's weaknesses, thereby encouraging them. Linda does more than acquiesce in her husband's faults; she encourages him to dream.

So Willy does not dream alone. He is the victim of Linda's ambition as well as his own. Just as Willy unconsciously projects Biff against reality as a living vindication of himself as man and father, so Linda projects Willy as her own ideal of all that a man should be, an ideal she must foster, protect, and defend if she is to be secure and, perhaps, tolerate the husband she has married. Contrary to the rules for good business, Willy is pulling more than his own weight.

Ben is Willy's hero, his ideal of economic and personal success. When he points to Alaska, Linda dissuades Willy from going. Willy needs a Ben figure; but if he has him, he does not need a Linda. So she sees to it that Willy repeatedly turns back to her as his "foundation and support."

Linda is a strong support, therefore, not for Willy but for his dream; a support that Willy is all too prone to accept. She may be right in her judgment that Willy can never be a Ben, a splendid opportunist in dark jungles; but she will never admit that her "more than" love for her husband cannot sustain him either. So by making himself radically dependent on his wife, while at the same time being unfaithful to her, Willy hopes to establish himself as independent in society. But betrayal exposes the basic dishonesty of the entire marriage relationship; it shows Willy to be even less a man. His marriage is not a fulfillment, it is an emasculation. Willy in effect has been stripped of his true self. With such a loss there is more meaning than he knows in his lame excuse to Biff in the hotel room in Boston: "I was lonely; I was terribly lonely."

Some of the scenes on which this analysis of Linda is based are recollections from the past, a past that is portrayed as Willy's alone. But these memories are not invalid because they are only Willy's. While he is often self-inspired to prophesy the future, Willy is wholly incapable of modifying the past. It is apparent especially toward the end of the play that Willy can see better when he remembers than he can in his present consciousness. These recollections are ironically out of the control of Willy's dream. The past becomes the only reality for Willy, the only part of his world that we can trust.

Finally, Willy does not vindicate his suicide by an appeal to Biff's welfare alone. A constantly recurring epigram proclaims, "Because the woman has suffered." This is the only confession Willy makes which can imply a personal fault rather than an unlucky inability to find "the secret." Exactly what Linda has suffered is a failure, and the failure is Willy himself. He knows this instinctively and it only heightens his anxiety and his helplessness. When Biff in the final scene suggests that Willy come inside to Linda, he recoils and, "with guilt in his voice," says, "No, I don't want to see her." There is no consolation left in this marriage because there is no dream left, except Willy's dream of total escape. Reality has come home not just for Willy but for Linda too. At the grave she cannot cry because she cannot understand. She never has understood.

Is Linda a conscious instrument of Willy's undoing? Is she a plotter or a schemer? No. Like her husband, she is merely weak; she shares his fear of truth. They are both guilty of self-blindness and the refusal to know and accept each other.

Like all domestic tragedy, *Death of a Salesman* has far-reaching social implication. Its portrayal of ignorance of personal values is the picture of a muddled and perverted social world of values, caused by the refusal of its citizens to assert their own individuality. In such a world particular involvement is basically unhealthy. In such a world disillusioned men like Willy Loman, abetted by such wives as Linda, are always afraid to "take that phony dream and burn it before something happens."

Sister M. Bettina, SSND

Willy Loman's Brother Ben:
Tragic Insight in *Death of a Salesman*

In the thirteen years since Arthur Miller's *Death of a Salesman* had its spontaneous Broadway success, critics have often cited as a deficiency in it the lack of tragic insight in its hero, Willy Loman. "He never knew who he was," says his son Biff at Willy's grave; and by a like judgment critics can substantially discount the play's tragic claims.

But Biff's choric commentary on his father, like many other very quotable remarks in the scene of Willy's "requiem," is not quite true. Willy did struggle against self-knowledge–trying not to know "what" he was; but he had always a superb consciousness of his own individual strength as a "who." "I am not a dime a dozen!" he shouts in the play's crisis; "I am Willy Loman . . . !" And it is this very sense of his personal force and high regard for it which qualify him as a hero.

What turns this self-esteem into something tragic and self-destructive is his contrasting awareness that, in spite of his powers, he is not what he wants to be. Himself partially unaware that he actually desires simple fulfillment as a father, Willy dreams of being an important businessman, greatly admired by his two sons. He has misconstrued the ideal of fatherhood, confusing it with the ability to confer wealth and prestige. Because of this misplaced idealism– and his related commitment to the economic delusion known as "the American dream"–he seems not to have the stature of the traditional tragic hero.

That, as his son Biff says, Willy has "the wrong dreams" is certainly true. What criticism has to decide, in the light of the play's dramatic structure, is whether this common human defect does not increase rather than weaken his effectiveness as tragic hero.

Because playwright Miller has buttressed the basic realism of *Salesman* with strongly expressionistic elements, analysis of his play has to be made carefully. Willy's stage presence does not equal his characterization, as it would in a more conventional play. Instead of simply appearing in the events on stage, he himself–or rather, his confused mind–is the scene of much of the dramatic action.

Consideration of tragic insight in Willy, then, leads one to notice an expressionist device which reappears with the regularity of a motif in episodes taking place in Willy's consciousness. This is the stylized characterization of Willy's rich brother Ben who, when closely observed, takes shape less as a

Reprinted from *Modern Drama,* IV (February, 1962), 409-12, by permission of the journal and of A. C. Edwards.

person external to Willy than as a projection of his personality. Ben person-ifies his brother's dream of easy wealth.

Ben is the only important character not physically present during Willy's last day. He is on stage only as he exists in Willy's mind. But he is the first person whom Willy asks in his present distress, "What's the answer?"; and in the end it is Ben's answer which Willy accepts. As one critic summarizes it:

> Ben "walked into the jungle and three years later came out with a million"; Ben shot off to Alaska to "get in on the ground floor"; Ben was never afraid of new territories, new faces, no smiles. In the end, Ben's last territory—Death—earns Willy Loman's family $20,000 insurance money, and a chance for them finally to accomplish his dream: a dream of which they have never been capable, *in* which they also can only be buried: the old "million" dreams.[1]

Although Ben is dead before the play begins, the force which he symbolizes draws Willy to suicide.

Ben also stands out as the play's only predominantly formalized character-ization. That in him Miller combines realism with expressionism in a ratio inverse to that of the rest of the play seems another indication of his distinc-tive symbolic function.

The audience first sees him when memories of a visit paid by him some twenty years before push themselves into Willy's consciousness. "William," he boasts, "when I walked into the jungle, I was seventeen. When I walked out I was twenty-one. And, by God, I was rich!" This is the first insinuation of what may be called Ben's theme—the going into a strange country and emerg-ing with its wealth. Willy, who in this scene is a young father, triumphantly concurs: ". . . was rich! That's just the spirit I want to imbue them with! To walk into a jungle! I was right!" Ben, whom he has presented to his sons as "a great man," has confirmed his ambitions for them.

At his second appearance in Willy's memory, Ben again exults over his wealth, but this time he puts his brother on the defensive. He is now making money in Alaska and wants Willy to come into his business. Willy does find the offer attractive, and he hesitates before deciding that, after all, he is "building something" here in the States. "And that's the wonder, the wonder of this country," he goes on to exclaim, "that a man can end with diamonds here on the basis of being liked!" Ben repeats, "There's a new continent at your doorstep, William. You could walk out rich. Rich!" But Willy insists, "We'll do it here, Ben! You hear me? We're gonna do it here." He is still calling this when Ben, for the second time, abruptly disappears into darkness.

Willy next sees his brother after he has finally admitted to himself that he is

---

[1] Kappo Phelan, *"Death of a Salesman," Commonweal,* XLIX (1949), 520.

a business failure. And from this point in the play Ben functions as a symbol of Willy's dream. He no longer is a memory; instead he has become a force working in the present.

Willy has lost his job, is thoroughly defeated, and wants to talk over with his brother a "proposition" of suicide. At first seeming to dissuade Willy, making reluctant appeals to his pride, Ben gradually comes to admit that Willy's insurance indemnity is worth suicide: "And twenty thousand—that *is* something one can feel with the hand, it is there." Willy becomes lyrical: "Oh, Ben, that's the whole beauty of it! I see it like a diamond, shining in the dark, hard and rough, that I can pick up and touch in my hand." Ben's motif, riches waiting in darkness, is working in Willy's mind. He no longer believes he can make money in another way.

The play's crisis ensues and Willy comes to see that his son Biff loves and forgives him. More than before he yearns to give his son something, and Ben immediately reappears to recall the suicide plan. The idyllic leitmotif which accompanies Ben starts up in accents of dread. "The jungle is dark but full of diamonds, Willy. . . . One must go in to fetch a diamond out." Slowly he moves into the offstage darkness. "Ben! Ben, where do I . . . ?" Willy pleads. "Ben, how do I . . . ?" Finally he rushes off after him; seconds later he is dead.

Ben's one-dimensional character becomes a facet of the intimate psychological portrayal of Willy just as expressionism fuses with realism in *Salesman* as a whole. Miller uses Ben—along with the more conspicuous devices of skeletal setting, nonrealistic lighting, free movement in space and time, and musical leitmotifs—to provide a deeper realism than conventional dramatic form would have allowed.

Traditional drama implements audience-insight into the hero's problem by his own voluble awareness of it; tragic figures are more or less poetically articulate about their destinies, desire, and mistakes. *Death of a Salesman* however, forces a question as to whether insight in the hero is a dramatic end in itself or only insofar as it heightens audience-consciousness. For, in spite of its hero's foolish commitment to something so hollow that he will not even admit it to himself, the play's structure permits its audience to follow in the very action on stage the inexorable working of his mind. Thus Willy emerges as more than a pathetic victim of American society. Miller employs expressionism precisely to show Willy's struggle against self-knowledge, thereby pointing up his personal responsibility for refusing to estimate himself sincerely.

What Miller believes to be the basic impetus of any tragic hero—the supreme importance of his self-respect, even when he must lie to himself to preserve it—is, structurally and otherwise, the main concern of his play. *Salesman* studies the break-up of an ideal rather than of a man. But Willy's collapse will follow inevitably that of his self-image. His existence has come to depend upon belief in his ideal. Symbolically speaking, he has become his delusion.

Functioning in Willy's consciousness as a personification of this dream, Ben is a most important "minor" character, a projection of his brother's personality rather than an individual human force. Through him Miller provides for the audience a considerable amount of the tragic insight which, though never quite reaching Willy, manifests itself to him in the dramatic presentation of the workings of his mind.

In one way Willy's commitment to his dream typifies a necessary breaking of the laws of reality by all men: their construction of the tenuous ideals of themselves which truth by its very nature has to destroy. Willy, who will give up his life rather than his chosen image of himself, represents the fool in each of us. By that very fact, he must go the way of the tragic hero.

5. Style

Leonard Moss

Arthur Miller and the Common Man's Language

Throughout his career, Arthur Miller has shown a marked tendency to argue general propositions in colloquial terms. "Listen!" a character shouts in "That They May Win" (1944),[1] a one-act play about returning veterans: "We the people gotta go into politics. Politics is just another way of saying how much rent you'll pay; and how much bread, chopped meat and milk your food dollar will buy, and what you'll have to pay for Junior's new shoes! You have to go to those Senators and Congressmen you elected and say, 'Listen here, Mister! We're your boss, and you have to work for us!' " Later, of course, Miller became more adept at shaping an outlook with the mannerisms as well as the rational content of speech, but all his writing reveals his penchant for voicing ethical abstractions, usually of wide social relevance. This habit evidences high seriousness; unfortunately, it has also caused stylistic problems.

All My Sons (1947) illustrates those problems. The play, coming after the apprentice efforts, obviously represents a definite advance in Miller's ability to manipulate language. To the casual observer, the dialogue may seem to be simply a phonographic imitation of an undistinguished contemporary idiom, replete with clichés and slang. Especially in the opening scene, comfortable gossip connotes the sense of security conventionally associated with everyday family and neighborhood life. The talk—ingenuous, friendly, relaxed— duplicates the good-natured banter one might expect to hear in any Middle Western suburban backyard on a pleasant Sunday morning. But this deliberate banality encompasses more than mere linguistic verisimilitude: the common man's slangy syntax has been used for dramatic purposes. "The play begins in an atmosphere of undisturbed normality," Miller writes. "Its first act was later called slow, but it was designed to be slow. It was made so that even boredom might threaten, so that when the first intimation of the crime is dropped a genuine horror might begin to move into the heart of the audience, a horror born of the contrast between the placidity of the civilization on view and the threat to it that a rage of conscience could create."[2] Intruding upon the tensionless domestic world, with its chatter

Reprinted from *Modern Drama,* VII (May, 1964), 52-59, by permission of the journal and of A. C. Edwards.
[1] In Margaret Mayorga, ed., *The Best One-Act Plays of 1944* (New York, 1945).
[2] Author's Introduction, *Arthur Miller's Collected Plays* (New York, 1957), p. 18. This edition is the source of all quotations from *All My Sons, Death of a Salesman,* and *A View from the Bridge*; passages in this work and in *The Misfits* are cited with permission of the publishers, The Viking Press.

about want-ads, parsley, and Don Ameche, a terrible threat to tranquillity becomes increasingly insistent, finally bursting apart the innocent verbal façade. The deceptively peaceful mood evoked by trite speech prepares the stage for desperate war.

More dynamic language reflects the rising apprehension felt by Keller, the protagonist, and his wife. Their questions, idly curious at first become urgent, demanding practical solution: "Now what's going to happen to Mother? Do you know?" "Why, Joe? What has Steve suddenly got to tell him that he takes an airplane to see him?" "She don't hold nothin' against me, does she? I mean if she was sent here to find out something?" (This last question is answered with another query: "Why? What is there to find out?"). Comic small talk continues, alternating with the grave interrogation; Keller conceals his growing "nervousness" by performing as the homespun humorist: "I don't know, everybody's gettin' so Goddam educated in this country there'll be nobody to take away the garbage. . . . No kiddin.' It's a tragedy: you stand on the street today and spit, you're gonna hit a college man." But as his secret comes into view, such pleasantries only bring his terror into sharper relief. At the climax, the hectic dialogue mixes the antithetical accents of normalcy and urgency. Keller stubbornly disguises the truth, his wife frantically evades it, and his former partner's son persistently drives to uncover it ("What happened that day, Joe?"); at the same time, Chris and the neighbors, unaware of the impending crisis, cheerfully pursue avocations ranging from love to astrology. Finally, when Chris discovers his father's guilt, ordinary speech becomes unable to carry the intense stress by itself and must be supplemented with exclamation and violent action. Kate "smashes him [Keller] across the face," and Chris in "overwhelming fury . . . pounds down upon his father's shoulder" (author's directions). By the end of the second act, the son assumes the role of interrogator, with a vengeance:

> What did you do? Explain it to me or I'll tear you to pieces! . . . God in heaven, what kind of a man are you? . . . Where do you live, where have you come from? . . . Is that as far as your mind can see, the business? . . . Don't you have a country? Don't you live in the world? What the hell are you? You're not even an animal, no animal kills his own, what are you? What must I do to you? I ought to tear the tongue out of your mouth, what must I do? . . . What must I do, Jesus God, what must I do?

Contrasting in style with such outbursts, especially in the last scenes, are the moral declarations delivered by Chris and others. The author wisely avoided making the antagonist a formidable intellectual: Chris's theory on social responsibility is put in plain terms. But where Keller's arguments are relatively concrete ("Did they ship a gun or a truck outa Detroit before they got their price?"), those of Chris are often quite abstract. The extent to which the son is occupied in distilling general meanings from his experience will be readily apparent in a few excerpts:

I never saw you as a man. I saw you as my father.

Everything was being destroyed, see, but it seemed to me that one new thing was made. A kind of—responsibility. Man for man.

Once and for all you can know there's a universe of people outside and you're responsible to it, and unless you know that, you threw away your son because that's why he died.

I could jail him, if I were human any more. But I'm like everybody else now. I'm practical now.

No less than three other disillusioned young men announce their protests against the world's evil, reinforcing the moral position taken by Chris. Larry posthumously speaks his shame in a letter on learning of Keller's indictment. George has suffered from *his* father's disgrace: "When I was studying in the hospital it seemed sensible, but outside there doesn't seem to be much of a law." And Jim gave up the dream of becoming a researcher: "These private little revolutions always die. The compromise is always made. . . . Every man does have a star. The star of one's honesty. And you spend your life groping for it, but once it's out it never lights again."

These speeches of Chris and his colleagues in disillusion, though vague, do provide a rhetorical counterpoint both to the simpleminded banter prominent in the first act and the intense exclamation and interrogation prominent in the second. However, they divert dramatic interest from the protagonist to the antagonist. The son, whose function had been to present a mortal challenge to his father, usurps the principal role, and neither Keller's harsh defense ("Who worked for nothin' in that war? When they work for nothin', I'll work for nothin' ") nor suicide can compensate for this distraction from the central character study. Apparently Miller became overly intrigued by that recurring figure of his early work, a maturing personality who proclaims the interdependence of all men. As a result, he fails to exploit the contrast he had carefully detailed through the first two acts—a contrast between Keller's seeming neutrality and actual involvement.

Furthermore, concluding set-speeches spoken by Chris, Jim, and Ann are anticlimactic; they dissipate tension at critical moments, an effect entirely opposite to that achieved by the judicious alternation of comic and serious moods earlier in the play. After the cleanly decisive second-act clash between father and son, Chris's cynical, moralistic declarations come as a wordy letdown: "We used to shoot a man who acted like a dog, but honor was real there, you were protecting something. But here? This is the land of the great big dogs, you don't love a man here, you eat him! That's the principle; the only one we live by—it just happened to kill a few people this time, that's all. The world's that way, how can I take it out on him? What sense does that make? This is a zoo, a zoo!" *All My Sons* shows clearly what is evident in almost every play Miller has written—the habit of following a well-prepared movement to crisis with a digressive denouement. His desire to articulate substantive truth, here as elsewhere, often restricts a potent talent for expressing inward urgency through colloquial language.

The desire was controlled in *Death of a Salesman* (1949), a technical masterpiece. True, Miller employs some relatively simple conventions to unveil his protagonist, such as generalized description ("a small man can be just as exhausted as a great man;" "a salesman is got to dream"), but more sophisticated verbal methods are dominant in projecting personality. Willy Loman characterizes himself by the manner in which he speaks. "Well, bottoms up! . . . And keep your pores open!" he crudely reminds his extracurricular girl friend, in tasteless cant of the thirties. When he gropes for metaphoric originality he cannot escape staleness: "Because you got a greatness in you, Biff, remember that. . . . Like a young God. Hercules—something like that. And the sun, the sun all around him." His most pathetic laments are stock phrases: "Where are you guys, where are you?" he calls to his sons, "The woods are burning!"

Willy indicates his superficiality through hackneyed catchwords that advertise a business ethic based on "personal attractiveness." "Because the man who makes an appearance in the business world, the man who creates personal interest, is the man who gets ahead," he pontificates, in an aphoristic rhythm; "Be liked and you will never want." Childlike, he gains assurance by repeating his facile success formulas: "It's not what you do, Ben. It's who you know and the smile on your face! It's contacts, Ben, contacts! The whole wealth of Alaska passes over the lunch table at the Commodore Hotel, and that's the wonder, the wonder of this country, that a man can end with diamonds here on the basis of being liked!" (His wife and younger son echo the favorite magical cliché; Hap's compliment to Biff is "you're well liked," and Linda asks, "Why must everybody conquer the world? You're well liked.") Stressing the potent terms, Willy explains, "I realized that selling was the greatest career a man could want. . . . There was personality in it, Howard. There was respect, and comradeship, and gratitude in it." Even his sons' names—Happy and Biff—reflect his naive euphoria.

The Salesman suggests his moral immaturity and confusion in another way through his many self-contradictions when offering advice to Biff. Though he warns that " 'Gee' is a boy's word," he uses the term frequently. He shouts at his son, "Not finding yourself at the age of thirty-four is a disgrace!" but later adds, "Greatest thing in the world for him was to bum around." "Biff is a lazy bum," he grumbles; then, "And such a hard worker. There's one thing about Biff—he's not lazy." He gives this advice before the interview with Oliver: "Walk in very serious. You are not applying for a boy's job. Money is to pass. Be quiet, fine, and serious. Everybody likes a kidder, but nobody lends him money." A few lines after he cautions, "Walk in with a big laugh. Don't look worried. Start off with a couple of your good stories to lighten things up. It's not what you say, it's how you say it—because personality always wins the day." Memories of past conversations reproduce similar inconsistencies. He excused Biff's stealing a football from the school locker room: "Sure, he's gotta practice with a regulation ball, doesn't he? Coach'll probably congratulate you on your initiative!" Yet he soon forgot this excuse: "He's giving it back, isn't he? Why is he stealing? What did I tell him? I never in my life told him anything but decent things." ("Why am I always being contradicted?" he wonders.)

Still other techniques could be cited, particularly the associations operative in Willy's nightmarish recollections, but enough has been said to make the point that Miller's dialogue is most telling when it works by implication rather than by explication. Unhappily, that came to pass only briefly: after progressing from the apprentice pieces and *All My Sons* to *Death of a Salesman* and *The Crucible* (1953), Miller seems to have retrogressed to his youthful habits. *Crucible*, like *Salesman*, remains for the most part undisturbed by its oratorical passages; perhaps the playwright satisfied his speculative bent in the long historical footnotes. In 1955, too, "A Memory of Two Mondays," a one-act play, managed to sustain a successful interaction between lyrical and prosaic modes. But the narrator device in *A View from the Bridge* (one-act production, 1955; expanded to two acts, 1956) caused awkwardness similar to that in *All My Sons*.

The narrator, a contemporary version of the Greek chorus, establishes a rhetorical contrast with Eddie Carbone much greater than that between Chris and Joe Keller. His sonorous periodic sentences (with repeated connectives, in the Biblical tradition), his dignified diction, elegant imagery, and legendary allusion are obviously far removed from the protagonist's lower-class Brooklynese, and succeed in fixing Eddie's tortured, inarticulate protests in a rational perspective. But his poetic style and formal explanations reduce the impact of those protests. In general, Alfieri's eight appearances tend to divide the play into short, self-contained episodes, interrupting the cumulation of tension. Probably the most disturbing instance of this follows the climactic kissing incident, which is abruptly terminated by this static announcement: "And if I seem to tell this like a dream, it was that way. Several moments arrived in the course of the two talks we had when it occurred to me how—almost transfixed I had come to feel. I had lost my strength somewhere." The slackened pace must subsequently be revitalized with some melodramatic violence—the police raid and later the knife fight. While a chorus conferred great blessings upon Greek tragedy, Alfieri's contribution to *A View from the Bridge* seems seriously limited.

Miller's experiments with American dialects, often imperfect, are almost always intriguing and sometimes brilliant. *The Misfits*, however, a screenplay published in 1961, is undoubtedly the poorest product of the author's mature years. In that parody of the ordinary man's dream of living with extraordinary style, common speech loses its incisive force; if *Death of a Salesman* is meaningfully colloquial, *The Misfits* is incoherently so. He intended the work, Miller comments in a prefatory note, to "have the peculiar immediacy of image and the reflective possibilities of the written word." What "peculiar immediacy" this "story conceived as a film" possesses appears mainly in the impressionistic locale descriptions of Reno and its desert environs. As soon as the dramatist, in his fanciful role as movie creator, turns from designing scenery to directing actors, he gives the set over to his lifelong antagonist—"the reflective possibilities of the written word."

Introductory personality summaries help to establish this precedence. At best poor substitutes for self-exposition, they can confuse rather than spur the imagination. Guido, one is informed, looks like "a football-playing poet." Concerning Roslyn, a "golden girl" who "comes bursting out of the closet, zipping up her dress," the reader must be able to assimilate the fact that "quick as she is, a certain inwardness lies coiled in her gaze," that "a part of her is totally alone, like a little child in a new school, mystified as to how it got here and passionately looking for a friendly face." And the male lead conveys the impression, somehow, "that he does not expect very much, but that he sets the rhythm for whoever he walks with because he cannot follow. And he has no desire to lead."

The dialogue is as vaguely abstract as these labels. Consistent with her ingenuousness, Roslyn does pronounce a few refreshing observations. "Birds must be brave to live out here," she exclaims, gazing skyward, "Especially at night. . . . Whereas they're so small, you know?" And this on lettuce: "How tiny those seeds were—and still they know they're supposed to be lettuces!" (It seems likely that Miller modeled Roslyn's oral charm, among other personal attributes, after the late, celebrated actress to whom he was married at the time he wrote the screenplay and for whom he intended the female lead.) But when she reflects on human life, her constant attempt to derive objective evaluations from her sense impressions transforms her youthful wonderment into adolescent preciosity. "All the husbands and all the wives are dying every minute, and they are not teaching one another what they really know," she solemnly tells Guido. Later she asks, "Oh, Gay, what is there? Do you know? What is there that stays?" Even her hysterical outcry during the roundup, perhaps her most credible moment, abounds in unclear generalizations: "Big man! You're only living when you can watch something die! . . . You know everyting except what it feels like to be alive. You're three dear, sweet dead man."

Similarly, Gay's words, especially at critical moments, are not merely trite, which is appropriate, but meaningless, which is dull. Enjoying the cowboy's existence Biff Loman aspired to, Gay Langland wants to be "free" to "just live." He knows what he is ("damn good man"), respects the same quality in other males, and in his Western drawl does his best to explain the rationale of horse-roping, bull-riding, and woman-taming. He feels obliged to communicate his awareness of masculine ambitions and satisfactions: "Maybe the only thing is . . . the knowin.' 'Cause I know you now, Roslyn, I do know you. Maybe that's all the peace there is or can be. I never bothered to battle a woman before. And it was peaceful, but a lot like huggin' the air. This time, I thought I'd lay my hand on the air again—but it feels like I touched the whole world. I bless you, girl." The obscure references here make the vision inconceivable: at what point does he touch that "whole world"? What images define his knowledge and their rapport?

Guido also blesses Roslyn: "That big connection. You're really hooked in; whatever happens to anybody, it happens to you." The nature of this "big connection" must remain a matter of surmise. While lines spoken by characters who lack verbal fluency and mental acumen will necessarily be tentative or crude, they should be intelligible to the spectator. Striving to grasp universal truths, Gay, Roslyn, and Guido distort their assertion beyond recognizable shape. Their resolve to formulate a vocabulary of integrity produces language that is neither natural nor rational; the banality sounds counterfeit. Willy may be Lo-man, but Gay is No-man.

Arthur Miller, then, brings about an interplay between idiomatically authentic, emotionally intense, and ethically meaningful styles. Sometimes his concern for abiding principles unbalances this interplay; at other times, when prosaic talk configures grim subjective realities, his writing attains its greatest power.[3] Joe Keller's bluff statements resound with increasing apprehension: "Because it's good money, there's nothing wrong with that money." "What have I got to hide? What the hell is the matter with you, Kate?" Likewise, Willy Loman's commonplace constructions define inward states. "He won't starve. None a them starve. Forget about him," Charley advises in respect to Biff, and is answered with the poignantly simple sentence, "Then what have I got to remember?" And Eddie Carbone's contorted syntax conveys frightening turmoil as, ashamed and embarrassed, he futilely tries to dissuade his niece from marriage. In one passage, his words wander about in a

---

[3]In *After the Fall,* produced this year, colloquial language is of secondary importance for the first time in Miller's work.

sobbing rhythm before stumbling to their apologe petition:

> Catherine? I was just tellin' Beatrice . . . if you wanna go out, like . . . I
> mean I realize maybe I kept you home too much. Because he's the first
> guy you ever knew, y'know? I mean you could always come back to him,
> you're still only kids, the both of yiz. What's the hurry? Maybe you'll get
> around a little bit, you grow up a little more, maybe you'll see different
> in a couple of months. I mean you be surprised, it don't have to be him.
> [author's ellipses]

In lines like these, in which suppressed feeling threatens to burst the everyday
verbal façade, the common man's language becomes emotionally resonant.
That may be Arthur Miller's distinctive achievement.

Arthur K. Oberg

Death of a Salesman and Arthur Miller's Search for Style

Arthur Miller's place in the contemporary theatre is based so exclusively
upon the kind of social or public play he writes that the distinction of his
language has been given small attention. When a play like *Death of a Salesman*
has been considered for its speech, it has been dismissed as "bad poetry."[1]
Although both Miller and Tennessee Williams have had plays directed and
staged by Elia Kazan, critics tend to maximize the essential difference of their
writing. In the established image, Miller's art is masculine and craggy;
Williams', poetic and delicate. Such generalizations are not unjustifiable, but
they obscure problems that Miller and Williams share and have attempted to
solve in their respective dramas. For all of Miller's obverse comments on
poetic poetry or the mood play,[2] his entire dramatic career has been an effort
to get beyond a limited realism and a confining prose. Like Williams, he is in
search of a style that will allow for an unusually expressive speech. And his
use of a narrator in *A View from the Bridge* and his breakdown of time and

Reprinted from *Criticism*, IX (Fall, 1967), 303-11, by permission of Wayne State
University Press. Copyright © 1967 by the Wayne State University Press and the author.
[1] Eric Bentley, *In Search of Theater* (New York, 1957), p. 82.
[2] Arthur Miller, "Introduction," *Collected Plays* (New York: The Viking Press, 1957),
p. 12; "The Family in Modern Drama," *Atlantic Monthly*, CXCVII (April, 1956), 40.

space sequences in *Death of a Salesman* and *After the Fall* have been attempts at creating occasions when such language may be possible.

Miller's own comments and writings on the drama can be blamed for many of the unfavorable considerations that his dramatic prose has evoked. Miller is too harsh in insisting upon the differences between drama and literature. In realizing that a play is more than a verbal art, Miller in the "Introduction" to his *Collected Plays* makes his point at the expense of undercutting what importance a text does and can possess.[3] There is an uncritical and confused use of words such as "poetic" and "social" that conceals how much concern with a distinctive language Miller's plays reveal. A distrust of poetic poetry by Miller is understandable in view of the abortive verse play revival and the suspicion of audiences toward emotion and poetry, a suspicion evidenced by a drift toward *"indiscriminate* understatement"[4] in the theatre. But Miller's recorded devaluation of the language of a play is at strange odds with his continued excursions into finding an adequate stage speech in his work.

What the body of Miller's plays confirms is a situation that O'Neill found in the theatre many years ago and that continues to perplex the American dramatist—a lack of an established and available idiom. An interest in and employment of dialects—whether Irish, tough, sex, or alcoholic conversation[5]—became O'Neill's response to this situation. It recurs with slight variation in Miller's archaic Puritan speech in *The Crucible* and in his varieties of American localese in other plays. We are given dialogue that is different from what we are accustomed to hear, but always sufficiently recognizable for comprehension. Slices of life are presented that alternately provide us with the pleasures of hearing familiar speech and unfamiliar (or, to its users, *more* familiar) vernacular. Whereas Shakespeare's use of dialect only pointed to the presence of some standard stage speech in the background, its use by O'Neill and Miller indicates the contemporary absence of an established idiom. Back in 1923 Ezra Pound objected to dialects as "a usual form of evasion in modern drama";[6] but such a judgment ignores considerations of their decorum for particular plays and of the competence with which they are employed. And the continuing use, for example, of Southern speech and slangy colloquialism in the American drama reveals both partial solutions and impasses unsolved.

---

[3] Miller, "Introduction," pp. 3-5.
[4] Louis MacNeice, "Introductory Note" to *Sunbeams in His Hat, The Dark Tower and Other Radio Scripts* (London, 1947), p. 70. American Group Theatre in the thirties and Actor's Studio today, assuming that acting neither begins nor ends in speech, testify to the fact that even acting has been influenced by this drift toward understatement; on the assumptions of method acting see Eric Bentley, *The Dramatic Event* (New York, 1954), p. 173.
[5] Bentley, *The Dramatic Event,* p. 32; *In Search of Theater,* pp. 225, 232; Kenneth Tynan, *Curtains* (New York, 1961), p. 203.
[6] Ezra Pound, February 1923 Paris Letter, *The Dial,* March 1923, 277.

Miller comes to a theatre whose audiences are daily glutted with words from the commercial media. He accepts the embarrassment of audiences before emotive writing while affirming the right of the theatre to make people both think and feel. Although poets and poetry are joked about in several of his plays, language is undercut only so that it may be possible at all. Like Shaw or Arnold Wesker or Jack Richardson, Miller presents the poet as dolt or dreamer.[7] And, like them, he then goes on to use words as if he had forgotten the difficulties involved. In the face of the absurd impossibility of finding even adequate words, Miller drives on to accomplish what would seem not allowed.

If the situation in the American theatre is as complex and discouraging as has been indicated—the lack of an established idiom, the suspicions of an audience toward poetry and emotion—Miller's various attempts toward solving the problems of text take on new meaning. They suggest as extensive an experiment as Eliot's with the verse line. Although Miller's revision of *A View from the Bridge* ended his one attempt at using a verse line in the theatre, each of his plays and nondramatic works relates to a lifetime search for a distinctive style. Miller's approximations of Western speech in *The Misfits* and of seventeenth century speech in *The Crucible* solved this problem only for these particular works. Like Eliot after *Murder in the Cathedral*, Miller uncovers in his dramatic career an effort to forge a speech that would generally serve for whatever play he might happen to write. In *Death of a Salesman* and the plays that follow—with the exception of *The Crucible* whose style becomes an interruption, usable for one play—Miller picks up where the dialogue of *All My Sons* left off.

From Miller's earliest plays to *Incident at Vichy* there is a distinctive speech which, regardless of ostensible setting or background of characters, is based upon a New York idiom that often has recognizably Jewish inflection (e.g., the rising rhythms of "Does it take more guts to stand here the rest of my life ringing up a zero?").[8] Miller has an ear for speech that can be heard in any of the New York boroughs, for rhythms that have filtered down into Gentile conversation many miles from the city. Beginning with a particular speech, Miller arrives at something that approaches an American idiom to the extent that it exposes a colloquialism characterized by unusual image, spurious lyricism, and close-ended cliché. One has the impression of characters cheering themselves up with speech that is counterpointed by what we already know as audience about them. For Miller, it is a conscious selection

---

[7]An interesting consideration of Shaw's Octavius and Marchbanks as "unintentionally sentimental" is given by Kenneth Muir, "Verse and Prose," *Contemporary Theatre* ("Stratford-Upon-Avon Studies" 4) (London, 1962), p. 103.

[8]Arthur Miller, *Death of a Salesman, Collected Plays*, p. 212. Quotations from *Death of a Salesman* are hereafter given in the text and are taken from this edition.

from the speech that he has known and heard from childhood through which he exposes such discrepancies, particularly rents in the American dream. And it is in *Death of a Salesman* that he perfects this idiom to allow for a more successful revelation of complex character than in any other play he wrote.

The language of *Death of a Salesman* has characteristics that link it with all of Miller's work. Miller has a talent for using words and phrases as leitmotifs ("He's liked, but he's not—well liked"), for writing what approaches but is less obvious and shorter than set speech. Linda and Willy's occasional soliloquylike musings relate to the kind of patterned speech that typifies Miller's earlier and later plays:

The cats in that alley are practical, the bums who ran away when we were fighting were practical. But now I'm practical, and I spit on myself. I'm going away. I'm going now.[9]

No, no. Now let me instruct you. We cannot look to superstition in this. The Devil is precise; the marks of his presence are definite as stone, and I must tell you all that I shall not proceed unless you are prepared to believe me if I should find no bruise of hell upon her.[10]

Similiarly, prominent striking images ("He was so humiliated he nearly limped when he came in" [p. 211]; "All the talk that went across those two beds, huh? Our whole lives" [p. 137]), recall the earmarks of other plays, dialogue that hesitates between mixed metaphor and metaphysical conceit:

Frank is right—every man does have
a star. The star of one's honesty.[11]

This society will not be a bag to
swing around your head, Mr. Putnam.[12]

Quentin, don't hold the future like
a vase—touch now, touch me! I'm here,
and it's now![13]

You'd better ram a viewpoint up your
spine or you'll break in half.[14]

Miller here reveals three things: a knack of linking an abstract and a concrete in metaphor, a pressing of metaphor to visual incongruity or cartoon-like

---

[9] Arthur Miller, *All My Sons, Collected Plays*, p. 123.
[10] Arthur Miller, *The Crucible, Collected Plays*, p. 252.
[11] Miller, *All My Sons, Collected Plays*, p. 118.
[12] Miller, *The Crucible, Collected Plays*, p. 244.
[13] Arthur Miller, *After the Fall* (New York, 1964), p. 100.
[14] Arthur Miller, *Incident at Vichy* (New York, 1965), p. 31.

animation, and a perference for letting an audience bear away one or two vivid images in contrast to the *copia* of a playwright like Christopher Fry. While implicit attitudes toward kinds of rhetoric possible within a contemporary play would further link *Death of a Salesman* with the body of Miller's work, it is the particular density of a familiar Miller rhetoric that gives *Death of a Salesman* a feel that none of his other plays achieves. And the density is dictated by the enclosed situation in which the main character is found.

When Miller undertook in *Death of a Salesman* to present the plight of Willy Loman, he offered a reexamination of radical aspects of the American dream. The Lomans, never a family of adults, gradually and painfully attest to discrepancies in the American success myth, discrepancies that their lives from time to time can no longer hide. What Willy and his sons and what Charley and Bernard indicate in their respective failures and successes is the presence of arbitrary gods. Willy clings to them as he is beaten by them, and Miller's "Requiem" confirms them as a part of the territory. For Loman they are both equipment for living and vestments of death. As the play moves through its rhythms of euphoric elation and relentless despair, Miller employs a speech that would uphold these values by embedding them in outworn, formulated clichés commonly negatively phrased: "Never fight fair with a stranger, boy," "Nobody's worth nothin' dead," "No man only needs a little salary." But elsewhere there is language that draws near to "something of a poetic tinge," "a great air of something like poetry," "a kind of poetry":[15]

> The world is an oyster, but you don't
> crack it open on a mattress! (p. 152).
>
> When a deposit bottle is broken you
> don't get your nickel back. (p. 154).
>
> Everybody likes a kidder, but nobody
> lends him money (p. 168).

But even when Miller attempts to revitalize language we detect one and the same process here going on—the reduction of living to a set of adages, whether familiar or not.

There are two actions concurrently running in *Death of a Salesman* and related to this reduction of living to chiché. One is a process of exposing and opening up, showing differences in the characters' ideals and lives; the other, an undermining of their clichéd and commonplace lives. The first movement

---

[15]George Jean Nathan; Eleanor Clark; Harold Clurman, "Reviews of *Death of a Salesman*," *Two Modern American Tragedies: Reviews and Criticism of Death of a Salesman and a Streetcar Named Desire*, ed. John D. Hurrell (New York, 1961), pp. 57, 64, 66.

is most obviously reflected in images of stripping down that recur in the play. When Willy protests that "you can't eat the orange and throw the peel away—a man is not a piece of fruit!" (p. 181), he ironically confirms Linda's early adage that "life is a casting off" (p. 133). In context, Linda's words sounded only like readily available consolation, but the brute honesty behind them becomes clear in the remark of Loman's uttered later in the play. Willy's and Linda's lines, when played against one another from such a distance, force an honesty that much of their talk would hide.

Further dislocations in the American dream become prominent in Miller's reconsideration of the ideals of athletic prowess, male friendship, popularity, unpopular success. A society that jointly praises the democratic ideal and the exceptional individual is seen to be schizoid in its confusion of opportunity, talent, and abstract right. Against the process of exposing these often contradictory ideals, Miller sets the weight of the entire clichéd speech of the play. What the characters say is an effort in conservation, an upholding of a societal structure that has made it less and less likely for the small man to succeed. Social and economic statement is involved, but Miller goes beyond this statement in presenting Loman as a man not only trapped by his culture, but growing ineffectual and old. Willy and his sons have reached a time in life when they can live neither together nor apart. Although Willy's feelings of loss and impermanence are intensified and partly caused by his lack of success, his predicament has more complex origins. Willy is a man of slipping powers, locked in the past. Pathetically, in the face of declining earning power and approaching death, he would keep what he does not have and provide for what is not allowed.

The passages of *Death of a Salesman* using intentionally spurious, lyrical metaphor and suggestive of the kind of counterpointing found in Chekhov and O'Neill provide their own charm and force:

> That's why I thank Almighty God you're both
> built like Adonises (p. 146).

> Like a young god. Hercules—something like that.
> And the sun, the sun all around him. Remember
> how he waved to me? (p. 171).

Miss Forsythe, you've just seen a prince walk by. A fine, troubled prince. A hardworking, unappreciated prince. A pal, you understand? A good companion. Always for his boys (p. 204).

Such princely metaphor arises in moments of euphoria and functions much like the pal or buddy talk of Willy and his sons or like the dimunutive language which ironically becomes *more* sentimental in seeking to reduce the sentimentality involved:

> A small man can be just as exhausted as
> a great man (p. 163).
>
> Be loving to him. Because he's only a little
> boat looking for a harbor (p. 176).

Yet, for all this recognizably stylized speech which is reminiscent of other of Miller's plays, it is finally the fragmented wisdom of cliché, shored against Willy's ruin, that defines the language of the play. Miller relentlessly pins down by means of New York dialect, and with a talent akin to Pinter's, the shrinkage and simplification of living made possible by cliché. The Lomans in *Death of a Salesman* use formulated wisdom to hold off the night when they will have to acknowledge what they evade, unhappiness and failure. In contrast, Charley and his son use this wisdom to reflect the constricted perspective and unrestricted ambition often necessary in the pursuit of success. "The sky's the limit." "If at first you don't succeed . . . ." "One must go in to fetch a diamond out." "The only thing you got in this world is what you can sell." In their clichés, Miller's characters reveal both partial, pragmatically Puritan truths and denials of what an audience sees before their eyes—that all Americans cannot and do not succeed, that men do sometimes cry, that having sons is no guarantee of masculinity or success. Although Willy repeats that "the woods are burning," he refuses to locate what he only vaguely feels and knows. With the exception of those moments when honesty is pleaded for, Willy maintains and is maintained by speech that attempts to supply hope for a situation that excludes it.

Behind the reduction of living to a set of recurrent adages, we hear the helplessness, hopelessness, and frustration of words that can neither cheer Loman up nor improve his predicament. These timeworn phrases became useless and superfluous a long time ago. But they continue to be repeated, and almost religiously, by the characters in the play. Like a charm, they are an evasion and fear of redefining and delineating what has occurred. In the familiarly colloquial and deceptively self-sufficient clichés of the American dream, all is caught and held. The rhythms of the play, recognizably those of lower middle-class New York, could be heard across the country, with variations only in inflection and phrasing and specific cliché. In these rhythms Miller gives expression to a specifically American process or tendency to talk against facts of loneliness and loss, the fact of time-space breaking down under the pressures of memory and madness. He gives voice to rents in the American dream.

Unlike the plays of O'Neill or Williams where much of the power derives from "the cost to the dramatist of what he handled,"[16] *Death of a Salesman*

---

[16] Stark Young, *Immortal Shadows* (New York, 1948), p. 65.

relies upon a greater distancing and objectivity of the playwright. Whatever "otiose breast-beating"[17] occurs is either so subordinated to the play's elusive reticence or so much of an expression of a kind of emotional cliché that the impression is one of a succession of preverbalized states that were reinforced in the theatre by the poetic lighting, music, and staging of Kazan. As Willy and the other characters aspire toward greater truthfulness, they are held back by a stylized, cliché-riddled language that encourages evasion as it seeks to bring back a time when Thomas Edison and B. F. Goodrich and J. P. Morgan were still possible. That *Death of a Salesman* is both a document and requiem to this time explains the play's language, if it also provides a circular defense for that style.

However suitable the density of cliché finally is for Miller's purposes in *Death of a Salesman,* we are left with the general impression of a text that is undistinguished and flat. Arguments offered earlier for an intentionally spurious lyricism or for an unusual turn of cliché relate to moments in the play that are too few to absolve the longer stretches of Miller's prose. The play's text, although far from "bad poetry," tellingly moves toward the status of poetry without ever getting there.[18] Although the reasons given for this situation go a long way to explain the quality of the text, to let the case rest on the attitudes of the audience either toward poetry or toward emotion explains one matter only to ignore the power that the play continues to elicit on the stage. That the distinction of the play is not primarily verbal returns us to our earlier considerations of the achievement of *Death of a Salesman* as one of style—style as rhythm, rhythm as style.

As we noted, Miller in *Death of a Salesman* uses a stylistically clichéd language, based on the inflection of a New York Jewish speech and rising to a peculiarly American idiom, to reveal the disparities between Willy's pipe dreams and what has occurred; alternating rhythms of elation and despair dramatically and artistically realize what life less coherently and concentratedly presents. As a result, the strength of the speech of the Lomans resides in its pressing toward what it must never become. Never a poetry of full light, it is a prose characterized by clichés that guy rhythm as they create a style. Here, the distinctiveness of the play lies. In looking beyond the clichéd words of *Death of a Salesman* to the rhythms of the speech and to what the clichés would hide, we draw near to the kind of appreciation that vaudeville, another popular art, must exact—when what is central are not the words spoken but the "bounce" of the music hall line.

---

[17] Tynan, *Curtains,* p. 260.
[18] See the critical consensus in note 15.